SHIRLEY JACKSON CASE AND THE CHICAGO SCHOOL

SOCIETY OF BIBLICAL LITERATURE
BIBLICAL SCHOLARSHIP IN NORTH AMERICA

Kent Harold Richards, Editor

NUMBER 5
SHIRLEY JACKSON CASE AND THE CHICAGO SCHOOL
The Socio-Historical Method

William J. Hynes

WILLIAM J. HYNES

SHIRLEY JACKSON CASE AND THE CHICAGO SCHOOL
The Socio-Historical Method

SCHOLARS PRESS

Distributed by
Scholars Press
101 Salem Street
P.O. Box 2268
Chico, California 95927

The Society of Biblical Literature gratefully acknowledges a grant from the National Endowment for the Humanities to underwrite certain editorial and research expenses of the Centennial Publications Series. Published results and interpretations do not necessarily represent the view of the Endowment.

© 1981
Society of Biblical Literature

Library of Congress Cataloging in Publication Data

Hynes, William J.
    Shirley Jackson Case and the Chicago School.

(Biblical Scholarship in North America/Society of Biblical Literature ; no. 5) (ISSN 0277-0474)
    Bibliography: p.
    1. Chicago school of theology. 2. Case, Shirley Jackson, 1872–1947. I. Title. II. Series: Biblical scholarship in North America ; no. 5.
BT30.U6H95   230   81–8973
ISBN 0–89130–510–6 pbk.   AACR2

Printed in the United States of America
1   2   3   4   5
Edwards Brothers, Inc.
Ann Arbor, Michigan 48106

DEDICATION

To my father who knew that people are the prime reality of this life:
William James Hynes Sr. (1893–1972)

SHIRLEY JACKSON CASE
(1872–1947)

TABLE OF CONTENTS

PREFACE

During the first two decades of this century there raged a religious battle across America no less fierce than the religious wars of the post-Reformation. At issue was not any particular doctrinal formula so much as the nature of the relationship between Christianity and the methodology of modernity, the scientific method. This same issue had surfaced at the end of the previous century within European Catholicism only to be quickly suppressed by the fiat of papal condemnation. In America, however, the issue was not to be so easily resolved and ultimately it caused the radical dismemberment of evangelical protestantism into two hostile camps: the fundamentalists and the modernists.

At the center of the modernists camp was a group of scholars assembled at the Divinity School of the University of Chicago between 1914 and 1938. This intellectual nucleus of modernists fought quietly in their classrooms and scholarly writings as well as publicly on Chautauqua platforms and in the popular media to maintain a creative interplay between science and religion. The fundamentalists saw such a relationship as a Faustian bargain. However, the modernists, in the tradition of Marcus Aurelius and Thomas Aquinas, found no essential conflict between the laws of science and of religion. This central disagreement brought these two groups into vigorous, if formally bloodless, battle. In this venture, the modernists were able to ally themselves in a united front with a number of prominent progressives. Thus when Clarence Darrow went off to do battle with William Jennings Bryan at Dayton, Tennessee, he was well armed with intellectual ammunition from his Chicago compatriots from "across the Midway." With an eye to more long-range ecclesiastical and educational reform, these same Chicago modernists carefully trained several generations of scholars in the most modern and scientific methods of the study of religion. So it was that a significant wave of modernism spread outward from Chicago, altering policy and polity.

As Charles Darwin had used science to reveal that humanity was the product of an extremely lengthy evolutionary process, the Chicago figures argued that scientific historical investigation revealed that Christianity was similarly a product of its own parallel evolutionary process. They were persuaded that in either case the handiwork of God was not diminished but shown to be more intricate and complex than first imagined. Accordingly, Christianity was understood as the product of the long continuous social history of believers working out their beliefs within different cultural contexts and under diverse social pressures.

Nearly half a century later there has been a notable renaissance of scholarly interest and research about the Chicago School, specifically the methodology utilized within the areas of New Testament, church history and theology. While this method has been variously named, the most common label has been the "socio-historical method." The two figures most intimately associated with this method were Shirley Jackson Case (1872–1947) and Shailer Mathews (1863–1941).

The existence of this renaissance of interest is evidenced in the spate of works from the Chicago School which have been reprinted recently, numerous scholarly references to the school in journals and professional papers, as well as the continuing interest generated by surviving members of the original Chicago School and their linear, if not necessarily ideological, descendants at the present Divinity School of the University of Chicago.[1] The variety of statements and claims made about the supposed nature and status of the socio-historical method has served to highlight the pressing need for a thorough examination and assessment of the socio-historical method. What

---

[1] This renaissance of scholarly interest in the Chicago School can be noted in several areas: (a) The number of works of such Chicago figures as S. J. Case and Shailer Mathews which have recently been reprinted. Case's *The Evolution of Early Christianity* was republished in 1952 by the University of Chicago Press. Two different reprints of Case's *Jesus: A New Biography* have appeared, the first in 1968 by Greenwood Press and the second in 1969 by AMS Press. The latter press also reprinted Mathews's *Faith of Modernism* in 1970. In the same year, Kinnikat Press reprinted the Case Festschrift entitled *Environmental Factors in Christian History*. (b) Various papers have been presented in this area to professional conventions, e.g., Robert Funk, "Shirley Jackson Case: Notes Toward an Appreciation," Society of Biblical Literature, 1967; Allan Gragg, "Philosophy of Religion versus Theology in the Thought of George Burman Foster," American Academy of Religion, 1969. A conference entitled "Consultation on the Chicago School" was held at Vanderbilt University in 1969, with papers offered by James Luther Adams, E. C. Colwell, Robert Funk, Bernard Meland, Wilhelm Pauck and others. Since then other professional papers have appeared including William J. Hynes, "The Socio-Historical Method of the Chicago School," Midwest Region of the American Academy of Religion, 1970; William J. Hynes, "Shirley Jackson Case: History & Hermeneutics," Society of Biblical Literature and American Academy of Religion, 1971; Larry E. Axel, "Modernism and the 'Chicago School' of Theology," American Academy of Religion, 1974; Robert Funk, "The Watershed of the American Biblical Tradition," Society of Biblical Literature, 1975. The last paper is an updated version of an address of similar title originally offered at the Vanderbilt Consultation. Unless otherwise noted, all references in this work will be to the earlier Vanderbilt version. (c) Within the present University of Chicago Divinity School itself: Bernard Meland, *Realities of Faith* (New York: Oxford Press, 1962) 109–112, 248–251; Bernard Meland, "A Long Look at the Divinity School and Its Present Crisis," *Criterion* 1/2 (1962) 21–30; John Knox, "A Few Memories and A Great Debt," *Criterion* 5/2 (1966) 24–27; Charles Harvey Arnold, *Near the Edge of Battle* (Chicago: Divinity School Association, 1966); Coert Rylaarsdam, "The Chicago School—And After," *Transition in Biblical Studies*, ed. Coert Rylaarsdam (Chicago: University of Chicago, 1968) 1–16; Sidney Mead, "Character and Continuity," *Criterion* 9/2 (1970) 25–27; Charles Harvey Arnold, *God Before You and Behind You: The Hyde Park Union Church Through a Century 1874–1974* (Chicago: The Hyde Park Union Church, 1974).

precisely was this method? From what sources did it spring? What ultimately happened to it?

The current work seeks to fill this lacuna by offering a systematic explication of the socio-historical method as understood and utilized primarily by Shirley Jackson Case. The majority of this work focuses upon Case rather than upon Mathews since on the whole Case seems to have been a more thorough theoretician of the method than Mathews. Thus Sidney Mead can view Case as "*the* representative of the socio-historical method."[2] Nonetheless, at pertinent junctures it will be necessary to compare the two men's employment of the same method. Once the method has been identified in some detail, close attention will be devoted to examining possible theoretical influences upon the method and its own inherent methodological adequacy.

Since it is the arrival of Case at the Divinity School of the University of Chicago which coincides with the rise of the Chicago School and the socio-historical method, the initial two chapters will attempt to give a brief picture both of what Case found when he arrived at Chicago and what intellectual horizons he brought to this venture. Specifically, the first chapter sets forth the central educational dialectic which was placed at the heart of the University of Chicago at its inception and which provided impetus for the modernists within the Divinity School to develop a method and a regime which inevitably brought them into confrontation with the fundamentalists. Further, a number of major discrepancies regarding the nature and membership of the Chicago School will be noted. The second chapter describes both the character and the intellectual development of Shirley Jackson Case himself. Surveying briefly the breadth and accomplishments of Case's career, this chapter will serve as a broader context against which to chart the evolution of the socio-historical method as analyzed in the next two chapters.

In the third chapter, the socio-historical method will be examined as it first develops within Case's early work as Professor of New Testament Literature. Here many of the central elements of the method can be seen. However, the fully delineated method had to await Case's later work as Professor of Early Church History. The fourth chapter will concentrate upon this development, concluding with a succinct profile of the socio-historical method as a totality. Particularly at this point, it is hoped that the reader may obtain a more precise characterization of the socio-historical method than has previously been available.[3]

---

[2] Mead, "Character and Continuity," 25. "The Chicago School was basically sociological-historical. In retrospect we can say that its creed was 'there is no sound history except social history,' and S. J. Case was its prophet." E. C. Colwell, "The Chicago School of Biblical Interpretation," Vanderbilt Consultation, 1969, privately possessed copy, 8.

[3] To the best of the current author's knowledge, only two previous works on S. J. Case's thought exist. One is Louis B. Jennings's "Shirley Jackson Case: A Study in Methodology" (Ph.D. dissertation, University of Chicago, 1964). However, contrary to its title, this doctoral dissertation does not attempt to characterize in either a precise or a synthetic fashion the socio-historical method

Major intellectual influences upon the genesis of this method will be assessed in the fifth chapter. A number of possible American precursors will be examined, including the pragmatists, William James and John Dewey; pre-Chicago School scholars, such as G. B. Foster; Case's own professors at Yale, B. W. Bacon and F. C. Porter; and so on. A variety of possible European precedents or parallels will also be investigated, including *Formgeschichte*, the *Religionsgeschichtliche Schule*, Ritschlianism, the work of Adolf von Harnack, the thought of Ernst Troeltsch, and others. Particular attention will be given to how Case and other members of the Chicago School viewed themselves in relation to these other men and movements.

Finally, the underlying assumptions of Shirley Jackson Case's socio-historical method will be more systematically assessed in the last chapter. Here conclusions will be offered regarding the inherent methodological adequacy and viability of the socio-historical method. It will be suggested that for all its manifold strengths there were several areas of crucial weakness which led to the diminution of its star in the face of more supposedly modern approaches.

The research for the current work is obviously centered upon the published works of S. J. Case and other pertinent figures. However, this research attempts to go beyond published sources in two areas: (1) extensive utilization of the notable archives of various members of the Chicago School, the *Journal of Religion*, and the American Institute for the Study of Biblical Literature; and (2) selective use of the oral history surrounding Case, the socio-historical method, and the Chicago School as made accessible through personal interviews or correspondence with such principals as John T. McNeill, Wilhelm Pauck, Sidney Mead, Bernard Meland, Ernest Cadman Colwell, H. J. Cadbury and Martin Rist.

The above-mentioned individuals figure centrally in the thanks which must be given by this author. In these individuals one sensed a certain shared gentility, careful craftsmanship, and Edwardian courtesy, particularly in the manner in which they took their valuable time to respond to the inquiries of one very much their junior in age and wisdom. Finally, exceptional thanks must be offered to those whose combined inspiration, support and critical commentary proved invaluable in the construction of this work: Harvey Arnold, Robert Funk, Brian Gerrish, Martin Marty, and David Tracy.

---

itself. Jennings's work concentrates on spelling out Case's views on the formation of the New Testament. The other work is Claude Martin Shuler's "An Interpretation & Evaluation of the Work of Shirley Jackson Case as a Historian of Early Christianity" (Th.D. dissertation, The Iliff School of Theology, 1964). This study which was directed by one of Case's students, Martin Rist, focuses mainly upon a comprehensive view of the content of Case's work in church history. It does not attempt to synthesize Case's socio-historical method as such.

I

THE CHICAGO SCHOOL

We could not be cloistered scholars:
we were to serve as a religious movement.
                    –Shailer Mathews

Harper's Dialectic and the Democratization of Knowledge

When William Rainey Harper (1856–1906) established the University of Chicago in 1892 and placed the Divinity School within it, he set in motion a particular dialectic which would later come to be centrally associated with that form of religious progressivism called modernism. One side of this dialectic was formed by Harper's wish that the faculty of the Divinity School should be professional, scientific scholars working in an atmosphere of guaranteed academic freedom. On the other side, he encouraged "a policy of maintaining a relationship with organized church life."[1] As Shailer Mathews, later Dean of the Divinity School, summed up the dialectic, "the Divinity School as an integral part of the University, had to decide whether it should become a detached school of religion or a leader in a religious movement. As a matter of fact, it chose to do both."[2]

This dialectic is clearly reflected in Harper's view of biblical languages, particularly Hebrew. Hebrew should be available to any intelligent and inquisitive person and not be allowed to become the exclusive domain of the scholar. In 1880 Harper had established one of the first correspondence schools in America, the Correspondence School of Hebrew, enrolling over 300 students in the first months. Renamed the American Institute of Hebrew in 1883, there were then some seventy professors of Hebrew and the Old Testament on the staff. The institute's publication, *The Old Testament Student*, was also retitled *The Old and New Testament Student* in line with a broadening of interests. By 1890 student enrollment had quadrupled

---

[1] Shailer Mathews, *New Faith for Old* (New York: Macmillan, 1936) 58. The story of the founding of the University of Chicago has been presented in much fuller detail in Thomas Wakefield Goodspeed, *A History of the University of Chicago: The First Quarter Century* (Chicago: University of Chicago Press, 1916) and in Richard J. Storr, *Harper's University* (Chicago: University of Chicago Press, 1966).

[2] Mathews, *New Faith for Old*, 59, 72.

and a general examination on the Gospels was administered to over 9,000
people.[3]

When Harper became President of the University of Chicago, this enterprise and its underlying dialectic went with him. He viewed the work of
such an institute as central to the general extension work which a modern
university should be doing for all the people. At this juncture the institute
bore the title American Institute of Sacred Literature, the name which it
carried until its demise in the 1940s. The University of Chicago Press took
up the publication of *The Old and New Testament Student* along with
three new additions, the scholarly *Hebraica*, later renamed *The American
Journal of Semitic Languages*, and the *American Journal of Theology*, as
well as the more popular *The Biblical World*. This institute and these publications would prove invaluable weapons in the impending battle between
the modernists and the fundamentalists.

Because Harper conceived of the institute's activities as properly part of
the extension work of the university, after 1903 the institute was administered through the University Extension Department. Harper had hoped to
establish a specific extension publication entitled *University Extension
World*. However, when by 1895 it became apparent that such a magazine
did not have the necessary market, Harper urged Albion Small to use the
allocated funds to begin the *American Journal of Sociology*.[4]

Going beyond its course offerings, which by 1898 had some 10,000 persons enrolled for 100 hours of study each, the American Institute of Sacred
Literature began a series of Popular Outline Courses in tract form, to which
most of the Divinity School Faculty contributed. In 1920 the volume of this
study material had reached over 560,000 pages which required some
600,000 hours of student work. At the same time over 50,000 pages of "tract
literature of constructive propagandist type were distributed at cost."[5] Much
of this study material and tract literature was aimed straight at the views of
the fundamentalists.

In 1916 the Divinity School faculty collaborated to produce *A Guide to
the Study of Religion*, which proved to be a very successful scholarly summary of recent methodological advances in the study of religion. Subsequently a series of practical handbooks was initiated. Harper's dialectic can
be seen reflected in the frontispiece of this series:

> This series of Handbooks is intended to set forth in a readable form the results
> of the scientific study of religion and ethics. The various authors do not under-
> take to embody in any detail the processes which lie back of their conclusion.

---

[3] Cf. "The American Institute of Sacred Literature," in Floyd W. Reeves et al., *University
Extension Services* (Chicago: University of Chicago Press, 1933) 129–137.

[4] Albion Small, "Fifty Years of Sociology in the United States," *The American Journal of Sociology*, 50/6 (1916) 786, n. 1.

[5] American Institute of Sacred Literature Materials File, University of Chicago Archives, 5.

> Such technical treatment is more appropriate for works of a strictly scientific
> character than for those intended not only to be used as textbooks and
> collateral reading in colleges and theological seminaries, but also to be of
> help to general readers. The volumes all seek to conserve the values of past
> religious experience. While each author is free to present his own conclu-
> sions, the entire series has the common characteristic of historical method.
> The editors have not prescribed any rigorous uniformity of treatment, but
> believe that the individuality of treatment will serve to stimulate thought
> and discussion. It is hoped that the series will help to show that the method
> of experiment and criticism contributes to stronger religious faith and moral
> idealism.[6]

The dynamics of Harper's dialectic were also embodied to a degree in
Ernest DeWitt Burton and Shailer Mathews at Chicago. Both sought to be
first-class scholars whose work played an essential role in their contributions
to the churches. Thus, during the first quarter of the twentieth century,
Burton held major positions within the Northern Baptist Convention. At the
same time Mathews' name became synonymous with the Social Gospel,
Progressivism, and the National Federation of Churches.

Mathews was himself particularly self-conscious and outspoken about
his advocacy of this dialectic, or as he preferred to state it, the need for the
"democratization of religious scholarship":

> The Democratizaton of an idea must have instruments and techniques. . . .
> In religion as in politics radicals have their place as irritants, but religious
> progress is possible only when religious groups are affected. . . .
>
> In the early days at Chicago we felt ourselves to be something more than
> observers or critics of conventional church life. We had a Cause, the exten-
> sion of correct, and as we believed, inspiring views of the Bible. We could
> not be cloistered scholars: we were to serve a religious movement.
>
> We had at our disposal two agencies for educational propaganda, *The Bibli-
> cal World* and the American Institute of Sacred Literature. . . .[7]

In Mathews' judgment American life was discernibly poorer for having
suffered "a rift between scientific theology and the rank and file of church
members."[8] This was a direct consequence of American theological students
having done their studies in Germany where they had been well schooled in
technical academic theology but not in the practical dimensions of the ministry. This rift between scholarship and the churches caused biblical scholarship to become inward and increasingly technical; in turn the churches
reacted against scholarly heresy by stressing the infallibility of the Bible.

---

[6] G. B. Smith, *Current Christian Thinking* (Chicago: University of Chicago, 1928)
frontispiece.

[7] Mathews, *New Faith for Old*, 72.

[8] Ibid., 42.

In seeking to overcome this schism, Mathews saw himself having a "vocation" as a "propagandist" in a "moral crusade" to democratize religious scholarship.[9] To this end, he traveled 30,000 to 50,000 miles a year, giving an average of 150 addresses annually, or nearly one address every two days! From 1912 until 1916, he was the President of the Federal Council of Churches. Beginning at the same time and extending until 1933, he also served as the Director of Religious Work of the Chautauqua.[10] Writing to Burton in 1915, Mathews described the pace of the summer at Chautauqua, New York: "We are having a great year at Chautauqua, but it is not exactly vacation for a poor brother who, like myself, is talking two or three times a day with the regularity of an alarm clock. I wish I were saying something but, at any rate, I am filling up time."[11]

However ideal Harper's dialectic may be in theory, this should not be uncritically confused with its attainability in practice. The accomplishment of even one of the two reciprocal goals could easily be a taxing enterprise for all but the most extraordinary individual. In the face of such a proposed dialectic, it could be questioned whether the relationship between these two goals is really that of a direct ratio where as one area receives attention so does the other. It could be argued that the relationship is far more normally an inverse ratio so that as activity increases in one area it must necessarily diminish to a similar degree in the other.

If Harper himself might be referred to as one of the most eloquent proofs of the direct ratio model, the examples of Mathews and Case may argue equally forcefully for the inverse ratio model. Thus, while we must credit Mathews with his highly energetic feats each year to promote the views of modernism, it is also true that this forced him to dictate some of his books between his breakfast and first class with the predictable result that not only did his academic scholarship suffer, but also his books sometimes display a lack both of proofreading and of consistent critical analysis. By the same token, if we grant that Case was less the peripatetic churchman and social activist, it is also true that most of his works are far better honed pieces of academic workmanship. Case is far more the chief theoretician of the socio-historical method than Mathews. Perhaps, after Harper and Burton, the embodiment of both sides of this dialectic no longer falls upon the back of any single Chicago figure but upon the School as a whole.

It was Harper's dialectic which ultimately led the modernist members of the Chicago School into battle with the fundamentalists. This intense conflict

---

[9] Ibid., 83ff.

[10] For an extended treatment of Harper's role in Chautauqua, see Joseph E. Gould, *The Chautauqua Movement: An Episode in the Continuing American Revolution* (New York: State University of New York Press, 1961).

[11] Letter, Shailer Mathews to E. D. Burton, August 15, 1915, Burton Letter File, University of Chicago Archives.

which raged through the nation, the churches and the courts would determine which side would win the "lay mind" of America.[12]

The Battle of American Evangelisms

The battle between the modernists and the fundamentalists was nothing less than a struggle over who would represent and shape American Evangelical Protestantism. Each side had equally emphatic, if contradictory, views on the inerrancy of scripture, the nature of God, the state of humanity, religious tolerance, the role of human action before the eschaton, etc. The full range of this battle has been amply chronicled and assessed elsewhere.[13]

The central issue of concern here was whether the relationship between religion and science is essentially a constructive or a destructive one. Because the members of the Chicago School were convinced that science offered an invaluable tool with which to understand religion and because they felt a moral obligation to share this knowledge as widely as possible with the general public, they were led into direct conflict with the fundamentalists. To the fundamentalists, science and the methods of science in the guise of biblical and historical studies were seen as destructive to the fundamentals of Christian belief. Not only were basic beliefs spun off as non-essential historical additions, but science was given a place of authority above Christianity itself.

Perhaps one of the first skirmishes in this battle occurred one week before the turn of the century, when G. D. Foster (1858–1918) of the Divinity School was accused in print of having offered a blasphemous prayer in the chapel. Foster was derided for having supposedly stated: "The doctrines on which we had rested for our moral and religious support are decaying, and it is necessary that they decay under such a course of study as we are pursuing here."[14]

Publication seven years later of Foster's most important and fairly radical work, *The Finality of the Christian Religion*, produced a more significant skirmish. Upon reading Foster's work, the Chicago Baptist Ministers Conference voted formally to remove Foster from their ranks, declaring

> Whereas a member of this Conference has issued from the University of Chicago Press a book, entitled, *The Finality of the Christian Religion*; Resolved that we as a Conference declare it to be our resolute conviction that the

[12] Meland, "A Long Look at the Divinity School," 27ff. Funk, "Shirley Jackson Case," 16.

[13] Cf. Steward Cole, *The History of Fundamentalism* (New York: Richard R. Smith, 1931); Ernest R. Sandeen, *The Roots of Fundamentalism: British and American Millenarianism 1800–1930* (Chicago: University of Chicago Press, 1970); also Roland Nelson, "Fundamentalism and the Northern Baptist Convention" (Ph.D. dissertation, University of Chicago, 1964).

[14] Roleit M. Raff, "We Realize, Our Father, That Our Doctrines Are in a State of Dissolution," *Western Recorder* (December 21, 1899) 2, as quoted by Nelson in "Fundamentalism," 118–119.

views set forth in this book are contrary to the Scriptures and that its teaching and tendency are subversive of the vital and essential truths of the Christian faith.[15]

Consequently, pressure mounted upon the Divinity School to disavow Foster's ideas. One minister pleaded with Shailer Mathews that unless Foster was censured the situation for moderately liberal ministers vis-à-vis conservatives would be intolerable.[16]

The heat of this controversy found the members of the Divinity School trapped between the two goals espoused by Harper. Clearly on the spot, they defended Foster against outside critics invoking the principle of academic freedom. Among themselves, however, they decried Foster's "destructive scholarship" which seemed destined to rupture their evangelical status with the churches. Perhaps implicit in Harper's goals was the renaissance axiom that "one is not obliged to tell all the truth, all the time." The goal of democratizing knowledge would need to be tempered by diplomacy.

When Dean Burton failed to win any agreement from Foster to be more circumspect and to temper his public speech, President Harper finessed the matter by arranging to have Foster transferred into the Humanities as Professor of Religion and Comparative Religions. Presumably Foster's bluntness, let alone the principle of academic freedom, would prove less troublesome to his colleagues in this area. In any event, subsequent complaints to the Divinity School regarding Foster's pronouncements were now answered not only with the reference to academic freedom but with the significant addendum that Foster was not a member of the Divinity School faculty.[17]

The advent of World War I, particularly the capture of Jerusalem by General Allenby in the spring of 1918, intensified this confrontation between two radically different evangelical approaches into heated hostility. For some unknown reason the premillennialist attitude of some of the fundamentalists, specifically that little could be done about wars until the millennium, sent the normally pacific Shirley Jackson Case into a scholarly rage. Witness the following from "The Premillennial Menace":

> Under ordinary circumstance one might excusably pass over premillenarianism as a wild and relatively harmless fancy. But in the present time of testing it would be almost traitorous negligence to ignore the detrimental character

---

[15] As quoted in Arnold, *Near the Edge of Battle*, 28.

[16] Letter, Reverend Lathan A. Crandall to Shailer Mathews, March 9, 1906, Divinity School Letter File, University of Chicago Archives.

[17] For evidence of the differing attitudes before and after the Foster transfer, see Letter, E. D. Burton to E. J. Goodspeed, January 2, 1909, Burton Letter File, University of Chicago Archives; Letter, E. D. Burton to H. M. Herrich, November 10, 1909, Burton Letter File, University of Chicago Archives. This was not the only time that Harper sought to resolve personnel problems through departmental transfers; cf. Harold E. Bergquist, "The Edward W. Bemis Controversy at the University of Chicago," *AAUP Bulletin* 58/4 (1972) 384–393.

of the premillennial propaganda. By proclaiming that wars cannot be elimi-
nated until Christ returns and that in the meantime the world must grow
constantly worse, this type of teaching strikes at the very root of our present
national endeavor to bring about a new day for humanity, when this old
earth shall be made a better place in which to live, and a new democracy of
nations shall arise to render wars impossible. While this struggle is demanding every ounce of the nation's energy, premillenarians are advocating a type
of teaching which is fundamentally antagonistic to our present national ideal.
Who is going to devote himself to a cause of which he is convinced before-
hand that it runs counter to the divine decrees and is doomed to failure before it is begun? At the present moment premillenarianism is a serious menace to our democracy and is all the more dangerous because it masquerades
under the cloak of piety.[18]

In the view of Ernest R. Sandeen, this outburst of Case contributed dramatically to increasing the level of *invective* between the modernists and the
fundamentalists.[19]

The fundamentalist forces rallied in a series of large conferences during
1918, producing the first World's Conference on Christian Fundamentals the
following year in Philadelphia. In 1920 the struggle between these two evangelical forces came to a head within the Northern Baptist Convention which
contained not only many of the leading modernists but also a significant
number of their fundamentalist opponents. The latter called a special Conference on Fundamentals of Our Baptist Faith to meet two days in advance
of the annual meeting of the Northern Baptist Convention.

> W. B. Riley, speaking on the topic "Modernism in Baptist Schools," de-
> nounced Chicago Divinity School and Crozer Seminary for their apostasy
> and claimed that many colleges were turning out students who could write in
> their examination papers, "It comes as a shock to the faith of many Chris-
> tians when they are compelled to face that fact that the Bible is not
> inerrant."[20]

This led to a resolution in the subsequent meeting of the Northern Baptist
Convention calling for an investigation into the charges of heresy being
taught in Baptist institutions:

> The resolution looking to the investigation of the teaching in our schools,
> colleges and seminaries created the wildest disorder. A sober, reverential,
> thoughtful body of men and women was transformed into a shouting, hiss-
> ing, applauding bedlam. The behavior was shameful. . . .[21]

---

[18] S. J. Case, "The Premillennial Menace," *Biblical World* 52 (1918) 17.

[19] Sandeen, *Roots of Fundamentalism*, 236.

[20] Ibid., 261.

[21] "Convention Sidelights," *Watchman-Examiner* (July 1, 1920) 834, as quoted in Nelson,
"Fundamentalism," 141.

This resolution empowered a committee of nine persons to gain evidence on the issue at hand by the use of questionnaires sent to all the Baptist schools. Many schools, however, including the Divinity School of the University of Chicago, failed to respond. It seems the committee lacked any power to compel such response. Nevertheless, the following year a "full" report was presented to the annual meeting of the Northern Baptist Convention, in Des Moines, Iowa. The committee concluded that only a small minority of Baptist teachers were teaching things inconsistent with Baptist views. This report changed little. Thus the fundamentalists continued to be displeased with the Northern Baptist Convention in general and the ongoing presence of the modernists in the schools in particular.

In 1921, several fundamentalist figures wrote the presidents of Baptist schools and seminaries asking them to purge their ranks of all such radical modernist influence. J. C. Massee, one of the most prominent fundamentalists, publicly accused Shailer Mathews and several other modernists of heresy.[22]

The intensity of this impending evangelical schism can be felt in a letter written by Reverend Cornelius Woelfkin, minister of the Park Avenue Baptist Church of New York City, to Dean Burton. The letter describes one attempt in 1922 to seek a coalition between the two sides; at a slightly deeper level, however, it reveals the increasing impossibility of avoiding a full rupture:

> Up to that time they had gotten nowhere excepting to stand on opposite sides, and a Mr. Rhoades of Toledo tried persistently hour after hour to get us to agree to some doctrinal statements which we all fought shy of. Finally Massee announced that he stood four-square for a static religion, a static faith, static inspiration, static revelation. I guess static everything. And shortly afterward I got up and said, now the real point is can we live together. The cleavage of the Denomination is focused right in this room. I stand at the antipodes of Dr. Massee. I believe in a progressive religion, progressive inspiration, revelation, methods and all things. I said that I regarded the hymns of John Greenleaf Whittier, George Matheson, many of Charles Wesley's and Frances Ridley Hvergal's are as inspired as the Psalms and much more inspired than some of them. Now is there room in the Denomination for Dr. Massee and myself. He shortly afterward got up and said that he considered my utterances as blashempy [sic].[23]

When the fundamentalist forces failed to win either control of the National Baptist Convention or the establishment of a creedal statement by

---

[22] Sandeen, *Roots of Fundamentalism*, 208. Steward Cole offers us a classic understatement in this regard: "The Divinity School . . . failed to win universal approval among Baptists," *History of Fundamentalism*, 90.

[23] Cornelius Woelfkin to Burton, May 18, 1922, Burton Letter File, University of Chicago Archives.

which the modernists might be condemned, they withdrew and formed their own parallel organization in 1922, the Baptist Bible Union, and established seminaries in direct competition with those of the modernists. This new group proved largely ineffective and was eventually immobilized by its own internal political divisions.

Within the popular awareness, there is clearly one event which was seen as the definitive battle between modernism and fundamentalism—the Scopes trial in Dayton, Tennessee, in 1925. At the symbolic level, the "Monkey Trial" represented a total confrontation in America between the forces of fundamentalism, biblicism and conservatism on the one side, epitomized by the silver-tongued populist orator, William Jennings Bryan, and the forces of modernism, science, rationalism and progressivism on the other, as represented by the civil libertarian, Clarence Darrow. Both men had felt themselves drawn to this classic confrontation. When each volunteered his services, the full potential significance of the confrontation fell into place. Each saw the trial as an unparalleled forum in which to debate before the American people the issue of whether scientific evidence for evolution and the religion of the bible were compatible or antithetical.

During the trial Bryan commented "I am simply trying to protect the world of God against the greatest atheist or agnostic in the United States."[24] Darrow returned the compliment several years later in his own autobiography:

> My object, and my only object, was to focus the attention of the country on the programme of Mr. Bryan and the other fundamentalists in America. I knew that education was in danger from the source which had always hampered it—religious fanaticism. To me it was perfectly clear that the proceedings bore little semblance to a court case, but I realized that there was no limit to the mischief that might be accomplished unless the country was roused to the evil at hand.[25]

The advent of this trial was a particularly significant moment for the members of the Chicago School. Here was Darrow, their fellow Midway resident, the close friend of Foster, who had once characterized Darrow as "the greatest potential influence for good in the City of Chicago," the perennial debate partner of Case, T. W. Smith and Eustace Haydon, battling

[24] William Jennings Bryan in *The World's Most Famous Court Trial* (Cincinnati: National Book Company, 1926) 299. The trial transcript was put into the book form by someone with a sense of humor who arranged the trial in a Genesis paradigm with the chapter headings of "First Day," "Second Day," etc. Of course in this case there was no rest on the seventh day as there were eight days of the trial.

[25] Clarence Darrow, *The Story of My Life* (New York: Grosset & Dunlap, 1932) 249. For examples of Darrow's religious views see his speeches on "The Myth of the Soul," and "Why I am an Agnostic," reprinted in Arthur and Liza Weinberg, *Verdicts Out of Court* (Chicago: Quadrangle Books, 1963) 417–436.

fundamentalism, the chief foe of these modernists.[26] In preparation for the trial Darrow met with Shailer Mathews and several other University of Chicago faculty to chart his strategy. Darrow invited Mathews to testify at the trial on the "relation between evolution and religion."[27] Darrow hoped to "introduce evidence by experts as to the meaning of the word 'evolution' and whether it was inconsistent with 'religion' under the correct definition of both words."[28]

Unfortunately, at the time of the trial Mathews was unable to testify in person. However, he sent a 500 word statement by telegram which Darrow read into the record with the following introduction:

> We expect to prove by Dr. Shailer Mathews, dean of the Divinity School of the University of Chicago, and one of the leading American authorities on the Bible, author of the book on "Contribution of Science to Religion," that "a correct understanding of Genesis shows that its account of creation is no more denied by evolution than it is by the laws of light, electricity and gravitation."[29]

Those familiar with the Scopes trial, particularly Darrow's examination of Bryan's belief in the inerrancy of the Bible, most often view the trial as a victory for the forces of liberalism. It is forgotten that Bryan's testimony was disallowed, that Darrow lost the case, and that John Scopes was convicted. The case was, of course, designed to be a test of the constitutionality of the Tennessee anti-evolution law. However, the Tennessee Supreme Court refused to rule on this issue while overturning Scopes conviction on a technicality.

Nonetheless, the quality of the debate caused people to perceive Darrow the victor. This was symbolically underlined by Bryan's death at the conclusion of the trial. Within the popular imagination of America, the trial was most often seen as a definitive defeat for the forces of fundamentalism over and against modernism.

As has been stated much of this victory was certainly at the perceived symbolic level. Certainly the Scopes trial did not signal an end to fundamentalism. If anything it rather marked the failure of fundamentalism to convince the American mind that the discoveries of science and religion were antithetical. The modernist position would become the credo of mainstream America. Henceforth, the position of the fundamentalists would be restricted to subsets of the American mainstream with subsequent attempts to influence the mainstream being largely reactionary and ineffective in nature.

---

[26] A. Eustace Haydon, recalling Foster's views in introducing Darrow, in Clarence Darrow, *Why I am an Agnostic* (Chicago: M. M. Cole, 1932) 35.

[27] Mathews, *New Faith for Old*, 228.

[28] Darrow, *Story of My Life*, 260.

[29] Clarence Darrow in *World's Most Famous Court Trial*, 224–225.

At a more empirical level, however, this victory and its specific dimensions have yet fully to be studied or chronicled. It would be extremely interesting, especially with respect to the history of intellectual ideas in America, to study what appears to be the slow but deliberate way in which the figures, scholarship, methods and arguments of the Chicago School influenced generations of graduate and seminary students, who in turn often assumed positions of influence within schools and churches throughout the country. Thus, while it has been noted that Chicago significantly influenced the ethos and direction of such other schools as Vanderbilt University and The Iliff School of Theology, no one to date has sought to document this.[30]

The collecting and interpreting of empirical evidence of this phenomenon awaits the application of the socio-historical method or the empirical research techniques of the contemporary L'Annales School. When this is

---

[30] Statements regarding influence of this type are most often of a general nature. With respect to the Chicago School's influence upon Vanderbilt, see Mathews, *New Faith for Old*, 81. The empirical study and documentation of such influence, although quite time-consuming, provides a clearer picture of the nature of such influence and the overall pattern of the growth of certain ideas within American belief systems and institutions.

A brief exploration of the archives of The Iliff School of Theology can serve as an exemplar of how such empirical evidence can be located and utilized. Through examination of faculty lists, it can be seen that this institution had a significant number of Chicago graduates on its faculty. From 1927 through the 1960s, at least fifty percent or more of the full professors were graduates of the Divinity School of the University of Chicago. In the late 1920s and early 1930s, a Chicago graduate was President of Iliff, Rev. Elmer Guy Cutshall. It was Shailer Mathews who gave the address at Cutshall's installation. Other Chicago graduates at Iliff included James Thomas Carlyon, Albert Jacob Behner, William Henry Bernhardt, Martin Rist, and Walter George Williams.

The academic bulletins for the 1950s at Iliff show lists of visiting summer school professors which read like a small Chicago School in exile, e.g., Donald W. Riddle, Ernest Cadman Colwell, Bernard M. Loomer, William Warren Sweet, Henry Nelson Wieman, and Harold R. Willoughby. Each year Iliff awards the Elizabeth Warren Fellowship to aid an outstanding graduate to pursue further graduate education. From 1926 until 1936, four recipients went to Chicago, three to Yale and two to Harvard. Since 1936, approximately an equal number have gone to Chicago and Harvard above all others.

On the ideological level, there is some clear evidence of the influence of the Chicago School on Iliff. In welcoming Martin Rist, a student of S. J. Case, to Iliff in 1937, the President of Iliff echoed a familiar Chicago theme: "This institution is committed unreservedly to an acceptance of the tested findings and the approved methods of modern science as they have been developed and applied to the interpretation of religion." Charles Edwin Schofield, "Presidential Welcome," Martin Rist Letter File, The Iliff School of Theology Archives. Similarly, there is a noteworthy letter from a later President of Iliff, Harry T. Morris, to a member of the faculty of the Divinity School of the University of Chicago, during the administration of Dean E. C. Colwell: "Dean Colwell understands and appreciates the fact that we share with your school your general point of view and your approach to a theological education. For a number of years there has been a close relationship between our school and yours. That is understandable when you know that most of our faculty have studied in your institution." Letter, Harry T. Morris to Ernest J. Chave, March 3, 1944, Morris Letter File, The Iliff School of Theology Archives.

done, this influence will be seen to be a complex phenomenon containing noteworthy convolutions and reversals. In the end, however, it will most likely serve to reinforce in an even more comprehensive way the statement of Robert Funk that "the Chicago School has probably had more to do with the victory over fundamentalism and biblicism in the Protestant tradition in America than any other single factor."[31]

The Chicago School: Method and Membership

There is no comprehensive agreement as to the precise meaning of the term Chicago School or what figures fall properly within this appellation. The most common view is that the term is closely interrelated, if not simply coextensive, with the phrase "socio-historical method." This is to say that both refer to a group of scholars at the Divinity School of the University of Chicago who initiated and practiced the socio-historical method. Such is the view held by such authors as A. C. McGiffert, Winthrop Hudson, Bernard Meland, and E. C. Colwell.[32]

A notable dissenter from this common view is Charles Harvey Arnold who sees the Chicago School as beginning before the advent of the socio-historical method with such men as G. B. Foster. In general Arnold wishes to extend the term Chicago School to include the majority of the history of the Divinity School. This means that it can be used to cover at least three very distinctive eras: (a) the era of the socio-historical method (1906–1926), (b) the era of the philosophico-theological method (1926–1946), and (c) the era of constructive theology (1946–1966). This view seems less tenable than the more common one which clearly distinguished between the Chicago School and the total history of the Divinity School.

Arnold's argument is based upon the assertion that the three eras he distinguishes are all "united in *mood, method* and *message*." The stress of unity in method is particularly problematic. With respect to the first era, in which he has included Foster, he states that "the distinctive unifying factor in the early Chicago School was the Socio-Historical methodology of its members."[33] Yet Foster's methodology is far from historical let alone socio-historical. Thus Foster himself stated to Burton: "I have been a systematic rather than a historical thinker, and while the defects in the former are evident even to myself, in the latter they must be glaring to you and the

---

[31] Funk, "Shirley Jackson Case," 15–16.

[32] A. C. McGiffert, "Chicago School of Theology," *An Encyclopedia of Religion*, ed. Vergilius Ferm (New York: Philosophical Library, 1945) 142. Winthrop S. Hudson, *Religion in America* (New York: Charles Scribner's Sons, 1965) 274–277. Bernard Meland, "The Chicago School of Theology," *Twentieth Century Encyclopedia of Religious Knowledge*, ed. Lefferts A. Loetscher (Grand Rapids: Baker Book House, 1955) 232–233. Colwell, "Chicago School," 8.

[33] Arnold, *Near the Edge of Battle*, 23–28.

naked eye."[34] Arnold is quite right to point to a continuity of concern between the first era and those which follow within the general history of the Divinity School. However, in fact there is not a continuity of method between these eras. Thus the method of Case from the first era is not the method of Henry Nelson Wieman of the second era, nor that of Bernard Loomer of the third era. As will be seen shortly, the socio-historical method is often avowedly antimetaphysical, whereas the methods of Wieman and Loomer are consciously metaphysical.

Within this work, the term Chicago School will be limited to those figures who employ the socio-historical method within the Divinity School of the University of Chicago between 1914 and 1938. These dates represent the most active utilization of the socio-historical method beginning with the publication of Case's *The Evolution of Early Christianity: A Genetic Study of First-Century Christianity in Relation to its Religious Environment*, in which the socio-historical method appears for the first time in full form, and concluding with Case's retirement. The latter date could be extended to encompass the continuing use of the socio-historical method at Chicago after Case's departure.

There is also no definitive agreement as to which individuals are to be considered members of the Chicago School. Within those who consciously use the socio-historical method, Arnold includes G. B. Foster, Shailer Mathews, S. J. Case, G. B. Smith, Edward Scribner Ames, and several others.[35] A. C. McGiffert includes Mathews and Case but leaves out G. B. Smith substituting instead J. M. P. Smith.[36] Bernard Meland leaves out Foster while including Mathews, Case, and G. B. Smith.[37] Winthrop Hudson leaves out Case while putting in Mathews, G. B. Smith, Foster and Ames.[38]

The question of membership is related in part to whether or not one is identifying the Chicago School and the socio-historical method with one or more specific academic disciplines. Thus, in various contexts, the Chicago School is spoken of as either (a) a school of New Testament interpretation, for example by E. C. Colwell and Robert Funk, (b) a school of theology, for example, by McGiffert and Meland, or (c) as a school of church history by Sydney Ahlstrom who sees a "disproportionate number" of this century's American church historians as being from the Chicago School.[39] Ahlstrom's list of candidates for inclusion in the membership rolls of the Chicago School is the most wide ranging, including such figures as William Warren Sweet,

---

[34] Letter, G. B. Foster to E. D. Burton, July 8, 1904, Burton Letter File, University of Chicago Archives.

[35] Arnold, *Near the Edge of Battle*, 28–59.

[36] McGiffert, "Chicago School of Theology," 142.

[37] Meland, "Chicago School of Theology," 232–233.

[38] Hudson, *Religion in America*, 276.

[39] Sydney E. Ahlstrom, "The Problem of the History of Religion in America," *Church History* 39 (1970) 230.

Robert T. Handy, James Hastings Nichols, W. E. Garrison, Winthrop S. Hudson, Sidney E. Mead, and Martin E. Marty. It is noteworthy that two first generation members are left out of this group, Peter Mode and John T. McNeill. The inclusion instead of a third generation historian such as Martin Marty may indicate that the term Chicago School is here being used in something less than a strictly historical manner and more in a thematic or stylistic sense.

Regardless of which of the above disciplines is identified with the Chicago School, the one figure who is almost always linked with the School and the socio-historical method is Shirley Jackson Case. Sidney Mead's judgment that Case is *"the* representative of the socio-historical method" has already been noted.[40] Colwell observed that the creed of the Chicago School was that "there was no sound history except social history" and Case was its "prophet."[41] Wilhelm Pauck has recently observed that "Case was undoubtedly the one member of the old Chicago Divinity School faculty who attempted to *use* the socio-historical method. He did not merely talk about it as Shailer Mathews had the tendency to do."[42]

Indeed it is Case's own scholarly odyssey from the field of the New Testament into church history and historical theology, when coupled with the widespread use of the socio-historical method throughout the entire Divinity School in the 1920s and 1930s, which helps to explain how three different groups can all claim the socio-historical method and the term Chicago School for their particular area of scholarly enterprise.

Ultimately any effort to determine particular figures or in any of all of these fields to employ the socio-historical method will remain severely hampered as long as there is no clear synthetic view of what constitutes this method. Accordingly this current work is intended to isolate and characterize specifically the socio-historical method as it is found within the work of S. J. Case.

[40] Mead, "Character and Continuity," 25.

[41] Colwell, "Chicago School," 8. Colwell refers to the Chicago School as "basically sociological-historical."

[42] Letter, Wilhelm Pauck to William J. Hynes, April 2, 1971.

II

SHIRLEY JACKSON CASE: THE PERSON

> The struggle toward renewal and growth is a fundamental law of life. Whether it be the skill of the hand, the power of the mind, or the sensitivity of the spirit, excellence can be maintained only by constant discipline. When lying idle, the deftest fingers lose their cunning. The wisdom of the scholar grows stale and musty with disuse.
>
> –Shirley Jackson Case

No methodology can be understood in isolation from either the people or the settings which have given rise to it. It is necessary to seek an ecology of any ideology. So too with the socio-historical method. The personality and intellectual development of Shirley Jackson Case is inextricably bound up with the genesis of this method. Accordingly, before proceeding to an extensive explication of the method itself in Chapters III and IV, this chapter will seek to state briefly pertinent biographical and intellectual *notae* of Case's career before, during and after his crucial presence at the center of the Chicago School.

Before the University of Chicago (1872–1908)

On a rugged farm near Hatfield Point, New Brunswick, Canada, Shirley Jackson Case was born to George and Maria Case on September 28, 1872. Throughout his life, this man bore the outward austerity of this land in his own personality and economy of speech.

After his death, Case's friends and colleagues often found it necessary to explain the discrepancy between this external cool demeanor and the inward warm person. William Warren Sweet at the memorial service for Case at Bond Chapel at the Divinity School of the University of Chicago remarked:

> Shirley Jackson Case was not easy to know. Many thought him cold and distant. It was constitutionally impossible for him to be a hale-fellow-well-met; he was never the life of the party and never wanted to be. He had no small talk; in fact he would not talk unless he had something to say.[1]

---

[1] William Warren Sweet, "Shirley Jackson Case: At Home and in His Study," Memorial Service, January 21, 1948, University of Chicago Archives, 1.

Ernest Cadman Colwell seconded this judgment: "The impression that he was an aloof, bitter, cold person is an entirely false impression. He was a shy, sensitive, friendly man."[2]

This outward reticence later gave rise to possibly apocryphal, if nonetheless revealing, stories about Case. Wilhelm Pauck relates the story that as Dean of the Divinity School, Case received a student in his study:

> The student showed up at the correct time . . . in the Dean's office. He was asked by Mr. Case to be seated. The student did. Case looked at him. The student looked at the Dean and was unable to utter a word. And after about two minutes, the student rose and said nothing. Case said "Goodbye."[3]

There is a clear overtone of this outward sobriety in the first article which Case ever wrote on the historical method: "Historical study is a sober science. . . . If one is a historical investigator he finds no delight in exploring freakish hypotheses, but will conduct a rigid research for the truth."[4]

Within the classroom, however, Bernard Meland indicates that this public reticence completely reversed itself: "There he was a communicator of the first order."[5] A tall broad-shouldered patrician, his thin face framed by long ears, white-gold glasses, and a half-irenic, half-impish smile. Case could be heard to admonish his students: "Don't believe *everything* you hear in my lectures. . . . Now and then I will give you some misinformation. I want to know whether you are thinking and studying, or just soaking up whatever you hear!"[6]

From his father, Case inherited a respect for hard work, cabinetry, and tools well-used. Sweet observed: "He early learned the right way to use tools and the necessity of accuracy and neatness; and accuracy, neatness, and sharp tools I associate with everything Shirley Jackson Case did."[7] Two years before his death, Case reflected on his boyhood experience of working an area which was not "composed of wide acres of smooth and fertile farms" like those in the Midwest. Instead, "here were steep hills and narrow valleys and stony plots of land whose fruitfulness had to be wrested from a grudging soil worked by the hand of man."[8] Out of this early boyhood experience grew the conviction that:

---

[2] E. C. Colwell, Comment at Vanderbilt Consultation, 1969, privately possessed tape.

[3] Wilhelm Pauck, Comment at Vanderbilt Consultation, 1969, privately possessed tape.

[4] S. J. Case, "The Historical Method in the Study of Religion," *Yale Divinity Quarterly* 4 (1908) 126–127. According to J. T. McNeill, this article seems to have been based largely on Case's inaugural address delivered at Cobb Divinity School on June 26, 1907. Cf. J. T. McNeill, "Shirley Jackson Case as a Historian," Memorial Service, January 21, 1948, University of Chicago Archives.

[5] Bernard Meland, Comment at Vanderbilt Consultation, 1969, privately possessed tape.

[6] Robert Maurice Bowman, "Shirley Jackson Case," *The Divinity School News* 24 (1957) 12–13. This is based on reminiscences of Case's teaching in Florida the year before his death.

[7] Sweet, "Shirley Jackson Case: At Home and in His Study," 1.

[8] S. J. Case, "Living in the Garden of Eden," *Crozer Quarterly* 22 (1945) 323.

> Man's place in the world is one of inescapable responsibility for the care and keeping of all the good things of life. Eternal vigilance is the price of continued possession. We are prone to lapse into the old Calvinistic delusion that the power and grace of God operate without reference to human effort. . . . Both divine and human providence are essential to the maintenance of a good world.
>
> The struggle toward renewal and growth is a fundamental law of life. Whether it be the skill of the hand, the power of the mind, or the sensitivity of the spirit, excellence can be maintained only by constant discipline. When lying idle, the deftest fingers lose their cunning. The widsom of the scholar grows stale and musty with disuse.[9]

These values so closely associated with farming were deeply enmeshed within Case's personality and went with him when he left the farm to pursue his formal education. He attended Acadia University, receiving his B.A. in mathematics in 1893 and obtaining a master's degree in the same field three years later. From 1893 until 1897, Case taught mathematics at several small schools in the New Brunswick area. After this he left Canada to accept a position in the United States teaching both mathematics and Greek at the New Hampton Literary Institute in New Hampshire. There he met Evelyn Hill teaching at the nearby Tilton School and they were married two years later.[10]

Although Case alluded rarely to his specific religious upbringing, it is known that he was raised a Free Will Baptist. The Arminianism of this group may help to explain Case's characteristic commitment to human freedom and responsibility over and against any talk of predestination. Even though his initial educational and professional interests did not center upon the formal study of religion, we find Case accepting an invitation in 1900 to serve as a part-time minister in a local New Hampshire Baptist church and receiving ordination to this end. The following year he left his teaching position to enter Yale Divinity School where in 1904 he received his B.D. For the next two years, he supported his wife and himself as an instructor of Greek at Yale while finishing his Ph.D. in New Testament under the direction of B. W. Bacon and F. C. Porter. Receiving his doctorate in 1907, Case accepted a post in history and philosophy of religion at the Cobb Divinity School in Lewiston, Maine. During this academic year, major articles by Case appeared both in the *American Journal of Theology* and *Biblical World*.[11] Interested by the scholarly promise already reflected in these first

---

[9] Ibid., 323–326.

[10] Most of these chronological and biographical details can be found in an excellent, if somewhat laudatory, biography which Case had the opportunity to proofread before his death. See Louis B. Jennings, *The Bibliography & Biography of Shirley Jackson Case* (Chicago: University of Chicago Press, 1949) 49ff.

[11] S. J. Case, "Paul's Historical Relation to the First Disciples," *American Journal of Theology* 11 (1907) 269–286; S. J. Case, "Authority for the Sacraments," *Biblical World* 29 (1907) 357–360.

two articles, in the spring of 1908, Burton, Dean of the University of Chicago's Divinity School, offered Shirley Jackson Case the position of Assistant Professor of New Testament Interpretation.

S. J. Case never produced autobiographical reflections on the scale that Mathews did in his own autobiography, *New Faith for Old*. Nonetheless, Case did pen one essay on this subject entitled "Education in Liberalism."[12] While placing himself intellectually within the perimeter of liberalism, he sought to avoid simple categorization of himself. Accordingly, his own position was described as a process of successive enchantments and disenchantments within liberalism. Because this description of his development is more thematic than specifically chronological, it is not always possible to match neatly these themes with particular dates in Case's life. Nonetheless, the majority of what is described would seem to apply to the formative years before 1908.

One of the earliest disenchantments which Case experienced with the liberalism he had received from the relatively tolerant Canadian Free Baptists was precipitated by the discovery, while attending a college sponsored by another denomination, "that character was quite independent of ecclesiastical creeds and ritual formalities."[13]

At this point and for some time after, biblicism in the key of lower criticism supplied the main staples of Case's religious outlook. This sufficed until the day he "began to wonder whether, after all, the eternal welfare of human souls depended upon knowing the exact meaning of a Greek preposition in one of the Pauline epistles or the shade of distinction between the *hiphil* and *hophal* of a Hebrew verb."[14]

Somewhat subsequent to this, Case began to adopt a more critical historical attitude toward Christianity. Initially, this was set within a strong Ritschlian framework which presumed correspondence between the religion of Jesus and contemporary faith decisions. At some point, this framework was supplemented by Harnack's distinction between essential and unessential aspects of past and present examples of Christianity. Nonetheless, Case's pursuit of historical evidence to substantiate these frameworks seems to have in the end led him to abandon the frameworks themselves. He became convinced that the historical evidence, with which he had familiarized himself, seemed to indicate that much of what had been central to early Christianity was not classified as central or essential to nineteenth-century Christianity as advanced by Ritschl or Harnack. Accordingly, Case found himself forced to conclude that this type of nineteenth-century Christianity was itself but another type of Christianity and also to judge that Harnack's distinction was less than productive.

---

[12] S. J. Case, "Education in Liberalism," *Contemporary American Theology*, ed. Vergilius Ferm (New York: Roundtable Press, 1932) 1:107–122.

[13] Ibid., 108.

[14] Ibid., 109.

Following in the wake of this disenchantment, Case joined forces with those seeking to formulate "a new conception of the nature of Christianity as a historical phenomenon."[15] This strong historical orientation shifted him away from the Ritschlian stress upon reduction and simplicity to a perspective which acknowledged historical variety and complexity. However, this approach was itself caught up short by the observation of the *Religionsgeschichtliche Schule* that many of the central beliefs of early Christianity seemed, in point of fact, to have been borrowed from other historical religious groups. In accepting this observation, Case found himself facing the alternatives by which he could avoid another disenchantment: (1) return to the essentialistic approach with all its contradictions, or (2) measure the religious worth of ideas not by their origin or uniqueness but by "their functional significance in the life of the people by whom they had been espoused."

Choosing the second alternative, Case determined thereafter "to know nothing about theologies save the beliefs and quests of real people."[16] Further, in order to judge the functional significance of these beliefs, he sought to understand the social and environmental situation of each group, its particular religious language, concerns, etc.

It is the development of this second option which results in Case's own historiographical and theological method, to which Chapters III and IV will be devoted. It is this method, the socio-historical method, which would seem to form the mature conclusion of Case's education in liberalism. This method would seem to differ substantially from the earlier stages in his liberal quest. In Case's view, all of these previous forays in liberalism had as their goal the finding of some secure religious absolute which was normative in character. However, the final phase of his intellectual development, as embodied in the socio-historical method, is based on the realization that:

> Every item in Christian belief at any period in history is a product of the experience and conviction of Christian people, and can be regarded as valid only so long as it serves adequately to express the sincerest convictions and deepest experiences of each new generation of Christian persons. This is the inescapable conviction to which we have been driven by the historical study of Christianity.[17]

Accordingly, no dogma can ever be absolute; "the only element of permanence in the process (of past Christianity) was the fact of never-ceasing

---

[15] Ibid., 109. There is no specific identification of the members of this group by Case. This reference might refer to any number of situations, including Case's joining Mathews at Chicago in 1908.

[16] Ibid., 113–114. This author's own evaluation of the influence exercised upon Case by the Ritschlian group, Adolf von Harnack, the *Religionsgeschichtliche Schule*, Ernst Troeltsch, etc., will be treated in Chapter V.

[17] Ibid., 115.

movement."[18] "Absolutes have been supplanted by relatives in belief; religious opinions of the past are not eternal, but only temporal."[19] The closest thing to an absolute or positional security was to adopt a "policy of aggressive action within the framework of an evolutionary world, i.e., seeking what is true for today, knowing it may have to be abandoned tomorrow."[20] This liberalism terminates in what Case will later call "human activism." This means that the responsibilities of defining Christianity will always fall ultimately upon the shoulders of the current contemporary person.

Case's autobiographical essay seems to presume a hierarchical scale of liberalism. Those who hold positions toward the bottom of the scale earn quotation marks around the term "liberal" or around the phrase "so-called liberals."[21] Fundamentalism would seem to be considered an aberration, totally off any such scale, as will be seen shortly. When Case places himself within this scale, it is always in a very critical manner given his own bittersweet experience with the variety within liberalism. The one term which Case seems to have been comfortable enough to apply explicitly to his own position without qualification was "modernist."[22] Thus, either this term or Kenneth Cauthen's phrase "modernistic liberal" would seem the most appropriate label to use for Case's position, other than identifying him with the socio-historical method itself.[23] Perhaps a somewhat less adequate term for Case would be "radical."[24] Sidney Mead's own term "scientific modernist" would also be appropriate since Case viewed the scientific method as central to the socio-historical method.[25]

---

[18] Ibid., 116. Case's statement here should also be compared with his views a decade later about the "vitality of Christianity" in his *Christian Philosophy of History*, see Chapter III.

[19] Case, "Liberalism," 117.

[20] Ibid., 116.

[21] S. J. Case, *The Historicity of Jesus: A Criticism of the Contention that Jesus Never Lived, a Statement of the Evidence for His Existence, an Estimate of His Relation to Christianity* (Chicago: University of Chicago Press, 1912) 1–31.

[22] S. J. Case, *Highways of Christian Doctrine* (Chicago: Willet, Clark & Co., 1936) 191–192. In the 1960s, it became commonplace to note how post-Vatican II Catholicism had been influenced by Protestant theology. It is interesting to note that Protestant Modernism of the first quarter of this century seems to have taken its name, if not is program, from the Catholic Modernist movement. In certain basic respects, both movements are quite similar, e.g., both were attempts to modernize Christianity from within, especially through the use of the scientific method, and both gave rise to strong repressionistic counter movements. For an interesting discussion of the connection between B. W. Bacon, Case's teacher at Yale, and Alfred Loisy, the Catholic Modernist, see B. W. Bacon, "A Summer Among Modernists," *The Independent* 69 (1910) 1208–1212. Also see William R. Hutchinson, *The Modernist Impulse in American Protestantism* (Cambridge: Harvard University Press, 1976).

[23] Kenneth Cauthen, *The Impact of American Religious Liberalism* (New York: Harper & Row, 1962) 148.

[24] Coert Rylaarsdam, ed., *Transitions in Biblical Studies* (Chicago: University of Chicago Press, 1969) 5–6.

[25] Hudson, *Religion in America*, 274: n. 16.

The University of Chicago and After (1908–1947)

In the fall of 1908, S. J. Case arrived in Chicago to join the faculty of the New Testament Department of the Divinity School. Case's immediate colleagues in this area were Burton, chairman of the department, Clyde Weber Votaw, Goodspeed, Henry Burton Sharman, and Frank Grant Lewis.

Under William Rainey Harper and Burton, the New Testament Department had been strongly philological in its orientation. Harper had died in 1906, while serving as the first president of the University of Chicago. However, the philological emphasis continued through Burton and later through Goodspeed. Although Case was thoroughly trained in the linguistic and philological perspective, his particular interest was the historical approach.[26]

Harper's death and Case's arrival in Chicago symbolize the beginning of a shift within the New Testament Department from the philological to the historical approach. Looking back on this six years later, Votaw explicitly acknowledges such a shift:

> When these advanced linguistic courses were first arranged by the New Testament Department, we had relatively few advanced courses in the history of the New Testament and in the New Testament theology. We have been adding, especially during the last ten years, a good number of such courses. For example, my course in the History of Interpretation, the History of Jewish Literature, the Eschatology of the New Testament, the Christology of the New Testament, Mr. Case's course on the Religious Status of the Graeco-Roman World, Mr. Goodspeed's course on the History of the Graeco-Roman World in the First Century. . . . These courses represent the shift in New Testament study from the linguistic to the historical and theological field. We have retained our former linguistic requirement, at the same time adding extensively to the historical and theological requirements for our degree. The need of substituting some of these historical and theological courses for the three majors in Hebrew, a major in Aramaic, and a major in the Septuagint, may appear quite clear.[27]

Robert Funk sees this shift as already beginning with Burton: "Within a common methodological frame, Harper and Burton established two lines at Chicago, the one [philological] which continued to predominate in American biblical scholarship, the other which became dominant at Chicago [socio-historical] but then died effectively in biblical scholarship. As a corollary, the one that died a scholarly death proved, in my opinion, to be a more accurate

---

[26] E. C. Colwell, "New Testament Scholarship in Prospect," *Journal of Bible and Religion* 28 (April, 1960) 202.

[27] Letter, C. Votaw to E. D. Burton, April 3, 1914, University of Chicago Archives, Burton Letter File. At this point, all courses dealing with Old and New Testament Literature were taught solely within the Divinity School and competence in such areas figured significantly in all degrees awarded through the Divinity School.

index of the emerging common consciousness than the other."[28] It could be argued that the credit for the establishment of the second line at Chicago may lie less with Burton, who himself was noted for his philological work, and more with Case and Mathews.

Once at Chicago, Case's scholarly career assumed two major emphases: (1) New Testament studies, especially as focused on the historicity and religion of Jesus, and (2) historical studies of Christianity, especially as focused on the problems of historical and theological methodology, the development of doctrine and the meaning of history. These two emphases are reflected formally in the particular faculty positions Case held within the Divinity School between 1908 and 1938. From 1908 until 1925, he held an appointment in New Testament interpretation. In 1917, he was also appointed Professor of Early Church History. He became the chairman of the Church History Department in 1923 and Dean of the Divinity School in 1933. The latter three positions were held by Case until his retirement in 1938.

These two emphases in Case's career were in a way a microcosm of a similar shift of emphases within the Chicago School as a whole. Thus, there was not only a shift from the philological to the historical within the biblical field, but also within the macrocosm of the Chicago School there was a further shift from biblical studies itself to church history and historical theology.[29] All of these shifts were represented in the rise of the socio-historical method. The socio-historical method seemed to develop initially within the biblical field and then to follow Case into church history and historical theology.

These two emphases in Case's career were also present in an overlapping fashion within his writings. Thus, Case produced articles and books about the religion of Jesus well after his move into the Church History Department. While still a member solely of the New Testament Department, Case produced several significant historical studies of early Christianity.

The outside observer cannot help being struck by the sheer massiveness of Case's literary productivity. During some forty years, Case produced over sixteen books, or better than one book every two and one-half years. He wrote over ninety-five major articles and nearly four hundred book reviews.[30] The authors reviewed by Case represented a veritable pantheon of

---

[28] Funk, "Watershed," 7.

[29] It should be noted that within the Chicago School at this point there was neither a strong differentiation between church history and historical theology nor between historical theology and the history of theology. Of the two figures most closely associated with the socio-historical method, Case was initially in New Testament and then in church history; Mathews was also in New Testament (1894–1905) and then in historical theology (1906–1933).

[30] For a complete bibliography of Case's books, articles, and book reviews, see Jennings, *Bibliography & Biography*. A less complete bibliography was included a decade earlier in the Case Festschrift, cf. John T. McNeill et al., eds., *Environmental Factors in Christian History* (Chicago: University of Chicago Press, 1939). Unfortunately, in the recent reprinting of the latter work, the later and more complete Jennings bibliography was not used.

the major theological figures in the twentieth century. In addition to all this, Case was editor of four different journals, including the *Journal of Religion*. Interestingly enough, the peak of Case's productivity occurs during the period of his greatest administrative activity. Some of Case's productivity is due in no small part to his consistent procedure of reviewing books in such an organized manner that these reviews would form the basis of future articles. These articles in turn were envisioned as chapters in Case's next book. This is the practice which Case advocated to Colwell: "Every article you publish should be on its way to becoming a chapter in your next book."[31]

In 1910, Case spent some six months of postgraduate study in Germany particularly at Marburg University. Unfortunately, there is no available evidence of what precise course of study he pursued at Marburg. However, it may be reasonable to assume that he used the opportunity to acquaint himself further firsthand with the work of such scholars as Adolph Jülicher, Wilhelm Heitmüller, and Walter Bauer in New Testament, and perhaps even the work of Wilhelm Herrmann and Martin Rade in systematics. Johannes Weiss had just moved to Heidelberg and Rudolph Bultmann had just received his degree from Marburg.[32] This particular year in Germany was also the occasion of various discussions and debates about the historicity of Jesus.

Returning to Chicago, Case drew on his experience of these debates, especially those at Marburg and Berlin, as the basis for his first published work in 1912: *The Historicity of Jesus: A Criticism of the Contention that Jesus Never Lived, a Statement of the Evidence for His Existence, an Estimate of His Relation to Christianity*. In the main, the work was a direct confrontation with and an attempted refutation of the mythical Christ of the radical critics, especially Arthur Drews' *Die Christusmythe*. Case rejects Drews' contention that a Christ idea, or "Christ of faith," was the primal formative element in Christianity rather than the historical Jesus:

> In the older strata of this literature the picture of Jesus is far simpler and more lifelike in a human way, while in the later strata of this literature more and more Jesus becomes the adorable Christ of Christian worship. Any treatment of this literature which represents the latter features as prior to the former, is sure to produce in the minds of those who give careful attention to the gospel narratives from the point of view of the literary genesis, the impression that to make the Christ of faith antedate the figure of the earthly Jesus is to stand the pyramid on its apex.[33]

In Case's estimation, Drews and the other radical critics let their a priori philosophical assumptions distort the documentary evidence. The remainder

---

[31] Colwell, "Chicago School," 5.

[32] For a discussion of the scholars at Marburg in this period, see Funk, "Watershed," 9.

[33] Case, *Historicity*, 296. For a more detailed discussion, see Chapter V, 115.

of this work was devoted to a detailed discussion of evidence for Jesus' existence inside and outside the New Testament. Up to the present day, this treatment of the radical critics and their work remains one of the most detailed and comprehensive summaries on this topic ever written.

This interest in the figure of Jesus persisted throughout Case's entire career, eventually resulting in a trilogy of books in this area. In *Jesus: A New Biography* (1927), he attempted to distinguish more expansively between the personal religion of the historical Jesus and the later Christ-evaluations placed on Jesus by his followers. The socio-historical method provided Case with the means to attempt such an exposition. It should be noted that *Jesus: A New Biography* was both his most commercially successful and controversial work. It went through numerous editions during Case's lifetime, selling in excess of seventy-five hundred copies. *The Historicity of Jesus* had sold only three thousand copies. The normal run of Case's works was between two thousand and four thousand copies.[34]

Some of the success of *Jesus: A New Biography* was undoubtedly due not only to its inherent scholarly worth but also to crafty marketing by the publisher. Twelve years earlier, Case had indicated that this work was "almost complete" and that he intended to entitle it "Jesus Christ: A Historical Interpretation."[35] However, in the context of the popular interest in the life of Jesus, as seen in such works of the period as Bruce Barton's *The Man Nobody Knows*, the publisher changed the title of Case's work over Case's own objections.[36]

Books on the life of Jesus continued to be potential best-sellers for some time after. Thirty years later, Edgar Goodspeed stated that his *A Life of Jesus* (1950) had sold six hundred copies a week and earned some $19,000 in the first three months of sales which he in turn used to purchase stained glass windows for the Divinity School chapel.[37]

The final book in this trilogy was *Jesus Through the Centuries* (1932). In this work, Case significantly broadened the historical content of the earlier term "Christ of faith" by tracing some twelve major historical Christologies which have occurred within the history of Christian thought. These Christologies were treated as theological interpretations of the meaning of Jesus arising from and designed for the needs of various historical Christian communities. The scope of this last work of the trilogy was another indication of the

---

[34] For a breakdown of the various numbers of copies of Case's works printed by the University of Chicago Press, see the Appendix. The number of recent reprints of *Jesus* has already been noted.

[35] Letter, S. J. Case to E. D. Burton, March 1, 1915, University of Chicago Archives, Burton Letter File.

[36] Morton Scott Enslin, *The Prophet from Nazareth* (New York: Schocken Books, 1968) xi–xii.

[37] Letter, E. J. Goodspeed to E. C. Colwell, February 22, 1951, University of Chicago Archives, Goodspeed Letter File.

author's own transition from New Testament studies to the history of Christian thought.

There is some belief that Case may have thought of adding a fourth book to this trilogy. Louis B. Jennings stated thirty years ago that "definitely in prospect at the time of his death was a new volume by Dean Case on the personal religion of Jesus."[38] Harvey Arnold has repeated this statement in his work on the Chicago School and Coert Rylaarsdam has picked up the statement from Arnold.[39] However, recent inquiries cast serious doubt on this statement. Charles Thrift, who was with Case during the last years of his life and to whom Case left his personal papers, is not aware of Case's planning any new book or being at work on any new manuscript: "I was closely associated with Dr. Case throughout his entire stay in Lakeland and I do not recall that he was engaged in any elaborate undertaking at the time of his death. He may have been making some preliminary notes for certain revisions in his book, *Jesus: A New Biography*."[40] After a fruitless search for any such manuscript in Case's papers, Thrift commented on the nature of the material left by Case:

> . . . there is nothing remaining among his papers that would be of any value . . . in explaining the development of his philosophy. The things that remained were largely personal items in which his wife was interested, and had little or no bearing on the development of his thinking. The sad story is that he destroyed most of his files when he moved from Chicago. He often expressed regret at the choices he made, both about what he disposed of from his files and his library. I recall hearing him say on one occasion, that if he had kept all of the papers he had destroyed, and destroyed all the papers he kept, and done the same with his books, he probably would have made a wiser choice.[41]

When questioned about his original statement, Jennings stated that Harold Willoughby had led him to believe that Mrs. Case had retained such a manuscript after her husband's death.[42] Mrs. Case died in 1962, and subsequent inquiries have indicated that she left no such manuscript. The effects that remained were placed in the hands of the Thrift.[43] This combined evidence would seem to make it unlikely that Case was, in fact, at work on any new study of Jesus at the time of his death.

The second emphasis within Case's career, the study of the historical development of Christianity, was evident already in his second published

---

[38] Jennings, *Bibliography*, 39.

[39] Arnold, *Near the Edge of Battle*, 49. Rylaarsdam, *Transitions*, 5.

[40] Letter, Charles Thrift to William J. Hynes, March 12, 1968.

[41] Letter, Charles Thrift to William J. Hynes, March 2, 1970. Since most of Case's papers seem to have been destroyed or lost, the single major source for locating his correspondence is the letter files of his colleagues, e.g., Burton, Sweet, Mathews, etc.

[42] Letter, Louis B. Jennings to William J. Hynes, January 30, 1968.

[43] Letter, Mrs. Egbert A. Case to William J. Hynes, February 29, 1969.

work: *The Evolution of Early Christianity: A Genetic Study of First-Century Christianity in Relation to Its Religious Environment* (1914). This work contained what may be the first example of the socio-historical method in nearly full form. It may have been the presence of this method which led Burton to comment to G. B. Smith in 1914 that this work of Case's was "for this country at least, a real path breaker."[44] This comment would seem to confirm in part a tradition about Burton's judgment on Case's work which Colwell has mentioned:

> According to oral tradition at Chicago, Burton's response to the book was singularly perceptive. At the next departmental meeting, Burton called the attention of the faculty to this publication of their younger colleague with the statement that in his judgment this method would be *the* focus of scholarly attention in the next generation. It was certainly *the* focus at Chicago; whatever was studied was sociological in method or content—or at least in vocabulary.[45]

With this work, Case moved beyond his study of Christianity as reflected largely within the literature of the New Testament toward a consideration of the variety of religious and philosophical influences present within the environmental situation of first-century Christianity. To a significant degree, this work helped to establish his reputation as a scholar of Christian origins. The quality of the work as reflected in Burton's highly favorable evaluation may have also played a role in Case's promotion to full professor the following year. This work and the socio-historical method evident within it will be examined in detail shortly.

Beginning in 1912, Case was given the responsibility along with G. B. Smith of editing the *American Journal of Theology*. The style of this journal was in strong contrast with another Divinity School effort, *The Biblical World*, which was edited by Shailer Mathews. In many ways, the different editorial policies of these two journals reflected the different personal styles of the men behind them. The tenor of the *American Journal of Theology*, like that of its editors, was cool, scholarly and generally less concerned with contemporary social issues. With respect to its content, it tended to develop along its own internal lines of interest or in line with current scholarly discussions. *The Biblical World* on the other hand, like its own editor, exhibited a far greater concern for relevant social gospel topics and was considerably more activist and aggressive in character.

Thus, when the United States went to war in 1918, Mathews' journal went along too. Accordingly, there was a special continuing series on "Preaching in a World at War," as well as articles by Mathews on "The

---

[44] Letter, E. D. Burton to G. B. Smith, October 1, 1914, University of Chicago Archives, Burton Letter File.

[45] Colwell, "New Testament," 201.

Moral Value of Patriotism," and "Religion and War." In addition, there were articles reassessing German values, such as, "The Religion of the German Kaiser," "German Freedom," and "The Paradox of Modern Biblical Criticism" which sought to show that higher criticism was really not German in origin. The third war number contains one noteworthy historical irony with respect to the pursuit of relevancy. The third installment of "Preaching in a World at War" was still running in November of 1918 when the end of the war forced Mathews to place it at the end of the number and substitute in its normal spot an editorial entitled "The Moral Perils of Victory." The editor had obviously found his concern for relevance outpaced by events.[46]

During this same period, the *American Journal of Theology* continued on its own customary path without outwardly reflecting any special concern for relevancy to international events. On the one occasion when Case deviated from his normal scholarly calm, by leveling an uncharacteristically strong attack on the social attitudes of the premillennialists at the beginning of the World War, he did this by temporarily immigrating to the pages of *The Biblical World*. The heated nature of this article, entitled "The Premillennial Menace," has already been noted in the first chapter. This article led one author to comment that "the fundamentalists apparently never cornered the market on invective."[47]

In a time of war, Case saw premillenarianism as fostering the unpatriotic and unproductive attitude that wars and social disruption were merely the signs of an impending millennium. Once the gospel had been preached, there was little else to be done. This is totally unacceptable for Case: "While this struggle is demanding every ounce of the nation's energy, premillenarians are advocating a type of teaching which is fundamentally antagonistic to our present national ideal."[48]

[46] Ozora S. Davis, "Preaching in a World at War," *The Biblical World* 52/1 (July, 1918) 3–15; ibid. 52/2 (September, 1918) 140–159; ibid. 52/3 (November, 1918) 248–263. Shailer Mathews, "The Moral Value of Patriotism," *The Biblical World* 52/1 (July, 1918) 24–40; "Religion and War," ibid. 52/2 (September, 1918) 163–176; "The Moral Perils of Victory," ibid. 52/3 (November, 1918) 225–226. George Holly Gilbert, "The Religion of the German Kaiser," *The Biblical World* 52/1 (July, 1918) 58–65. D. D. Luckenbill, "German Freedom," *The Biblical World* 52/2 (September, 1918) 177–184. Louis Wallis, "The Paradox of Modern Biblical Criticism," *The Biblical World* 52/1 (July, 1918) 41–49.

[47] Sandeen, *The Roots of Fundamentalism*, 236. Sandeen believes that Case's article exceeded even the normal standards of decorum for *The Biblical World*. The present author holds that Case's essay was very much in keeping with this journal's tenor and decorum especially with respect to the war numbers. The number in which Case's article appears begins with an unsigned editorial, probably by Mathews, which virtually rules out pacifism for Christians. Cf. "Piety and Religion," *The Biblical World* 52/1 (July, 1918) 1. It is also noteworthy that all of the academic departments at the University of Chicago were required by the War Department to demonstrate what members of each department were doing to aid the war effort. Cf. Letter, E. D. Burton to Conyers Read, June 11, 1917, University of Chicago Archives, Burton Letter File.

[48] S. J. Case, "The Premillennial Menace," *The Biblical World* 52/1 (July, 1918) 17.

Not satisfied with merely inveighing against the beliefs as such of this particular brand of fundamentalists, Case managed to dredge up an *ad hominem* argument of "guilt by association." Thus the extensive premillennial activity throughout the country has "a thoroughness suspiciously Teutonic" which raises the specter of "German gold" behind such a venture.[49] What could have evoked such an alarmed reaction from the normally taciturn scholar? What sensitive ideological nerve was so activated as to provoke the sweeping conclusion that the premillennialists represented "a pronounced enemy of democracy and a serious menace to the nation's morale in this hour of its need"?[50] Most likely these activities posed a direct affront to that central belief which Case had absorbed from his early association with the Free Will Baptists and which would become such an essential assumption of the socio-historical method—his deep conviction in the inescapable necessity of "human activism."

This premillennialism and accompanying apocalyptic interpretations of the New Testament occasioned by the World War led Case to publish three major works in two years in this area. Two were scholarly in nature: *The Millennial Hope: A Phase of War-Time Thinking* (1918) and *The Revelation of John: A Historical Interpretation* (1919). The third work was intended for adult education purposes: *The Book of Revelation: An Outline Bible-Study Course of the American Institute of Sacred Literature* (1918).

The curriculum design of the New Testament Department of this period can offer a further index to Case's scholarly interests. Whereas Burton and Goodspeed typically concentrated almost exclusively upon the literature of the New Testament, slightly over half of Case's courses dealt with Christianity in relationship to the different environmental contexts of the early centuries, for example, "Christianity and Contemporary Religions" or "Early Christianity and Contemporary Philosophy."[51] This interest is also institutionally reflected in Case's acceptance of a joint appointment in both New Testament Literature and Early Church History in 1917. This dual appointment continued until 1925.

In 1923, Case was named chairman of the rather small Department of Church History. In this same year, he produced a social history of the first-century church entitled *The Social Origins of Christianity*. A decade later, as he assumed the Deanship of the Divinity School, he expanded this theme in the Rauschenbusch Memorial Lectures: *The Social Triumph of the Ancient Church* (1933).

---

[49] Ibid., 20.

[50] Ibid., 23.

[51] Several examples of course sheets in which the responsibilities of the members of the New Testament Department are indicated in yearly cycles can be found in the Burton Letter File in the University of Chicago Archives.

During these administrative years, Case continued to teach as well as produce historical studies, such as *Experience with the Supernatural in Early Christian Times* (1929), the previously mentioned *Jesus Through The Centuries* (1932), and *Highways of Christian Doctrine* (1936). The latter represented a popular and less than fully comprehensive history of Christian doctrine.

In line with the socio-historical method's concern to study beliefs and institutions as generated by actual historical individuals, Case wrote *Makers of Christianity: From Jesus to Charlemagne* (1934), an early attempt to study Christianity biographically. He also edited two other historical works: *Studies in Early Christianity* (1928), a Festschrift in honor of B. W. Bacon and F. C. Porter of Yale, and a *Bibliographical Guide to the History of Christianity* (1931) to which Case himself contributed four chapters. The latter was a combined effort by the Church History Department in preparation for an on-site evaluation of the state of the teaching of church history in China, Japan, the Philippine Islands and India. The initial idea was that of John R. Mott, the subsequent financing that of John D. Rockefeller, and the consequent touring that of Case. It was understood that the books incorporated within the bibliography would be made available gratis to all of the faculties of church history visited. Returning from this tour, Case summarized the results in the *Report of the Church History Deputation to the Orient: September, 1931, to March, 1932.*

Under Case's management, the Church History Department grew from a relatively small and somewhat insignificant group into one which eventually eclipsed the New Testament Department. Whereas Burton could boast in 1915 that the New Testament Department was the "largest in the world," the Church History Department by contrast had from the beginning of the University of Chicago been very modest in size, rarely composed of more than two full-time members either under the leadership of the first chairperson, Dean Eric Baker Huber (1892–1907) or under the second chairperson, Andrew McLaughlin of the History Department (1908–1923).[52] When Case's regime began in 1923, the department consisted of Winfred Ernest Garrison, who had been an Associate Professor of Church History since 1921, and George Peter Mode, who had been in the department since receiving his doctorate from Chicago in 1914. By the end of Case's administration, this department had nearly trebled in size with historians of unquestioned stature responsible for the major historical periods. So pronounced was this growth in both size and quality that it could give rise to a parallel, if retrospective, boast by Wilhelm Pauck that "in the 1920s and 1930s [we were] the most powerful Department of Church History anywhere in the world!"[53]

---

[52] Letter, E. D. Burton to President Judson, March 2, 1915, University of Chicago Archives, Burton Letter File.

[53] Wilhelm Pauck, Discussion Vanderbilt Conference, 1969, privately possessed tape.

It may be that this growing strength, capped by Case's becoming Dean in 1933, was a contributing factor in the "intense academic feud" which existed between S. J. Case and E. J. Goodspeed. Those caught in the crossfire have supposed that the cause resided in either differences of methodology or personality. As will be seen in the next chapter, Goodspeed represented the documentarist's approach which the socio-historical method was intent to supercede. Ultimately their colleague Ernest Cadman Colwell concluded that "they were two antithetical persons."[54] However, the pertinent archives seem to reflect a warm, cordial relationship up to and through 1923, when Case became Church History Chairman and Goodspeed became New Testament Chairman.[55] Thus, the feud would have to have arisen after this and accordingly would not seem to be explained by differences of method or personality. Again such a feud may be more related to the shift in strength between the fields and the fact that the chairman of one, rather than the other, became Dean. Goodspeed may very well have anticipated becoming Dean himself since he was Case's chronological and professorial senior, a graduate of the Divinity School, and a member of a family intimately tied to the founding of the University of Chicago. To experience the intensity of this feud, one has only to view the spirited discussion between the two figures relative to whether or not Goodspeed had full faculty privileges within the Divinity School.[56]

It was Case himself who was often responsible for recruiting such new blood for this field as John T. McNeill, Mathew Spinka, Wilhelm Pauck, William Warren Sweet, and so on. Spinka joined the Divinity School and the Chicago Theological Seminary in 1926. To convince Sweet and McNeill to join the faculty during the following year, Case journeyed personally to Depauw University in Indiana and to Knox College in Toronto respectively. Dean Shailer Mathews offered consistent support in these initial ventures. Efforts to have Kenneth Scott Latourette join the group were unsuccessful. Although Pauck had been on the Chicago Theological School faculty since 1926, Case was unable to secure his move to the Divinity Schoool until the year after Case's own retirement.[57]

Once this group was assembled, Case exercised tireless husbandry supporting each member in his own scholarly pursuits as well as occasionally suggesting potentially valuable projects or joint ventures. McNeill recalled that it was a suggestion from Case which started him on his book on Calvin.[58] Behind the scenes, Case worked quietly to fend off faculty piracy

---

[54] E. C. Colwell, Discussion Vanderbilt Conference, 1969, privately possessed tape.

[55] See Letter, S. J. Case to E. J. Goodspeed, October 17, 1923, University of Chicago Archives, Goodspeed Letter File.

[56] Letter, E. J. Goodspeed to S. J. Case, April 2, 1936, University of Chicago Archives, Goodspeed Letter File.

[57] This is Pauck's own judgment, see Pauck, Discussion Vanderbilt Conference.

[58] Letter, John T. McNeill to William J. Hynes, August 17, 1970.

from without. An excellent example of this is a personal three-page, single-spaced, typewritten letter from Case to Sweet discussing the long-range advantages and disadvantages of an offer from Drew University to Sweet.[59]

This group also seemed marked by a special warmth, conviviality, and friendship. McNeill has observed that "we worked in personal harmony and in constant co-operation."[60] Sweet corroborated the existence of such an atmosphere:

> Dr. Case set for me and for many others an example of devotion to a high minded search for truth. His light in Swift Hall burned nightly, and John McNeill's and mine burned along side of it, and at ten o'clock nightly we three trudged home together. Dr. Case had brought us both to the University the same year, 1927, and there was never an unkind word or a misunderstanding between us.[61]

After Case's retirement, the Church History Department retained its general strength and vigor through the early 1940s. However, in 1943, Garrison retired and Spinka went to Hartford Theological Seminary. John T. McNeill went to Union Theological Seminary in New York the next year. Sweet accepted an appointment at Harvard in 1946. Only Wilhelm Pauck remained at Chicago through this decade. What had taken Case some fifteen years to assemble was lost in half as many years. Insofar as the Chicago School is to be identified with the socio-historical method, the attrition of faculty so closely associated with the use of this method may be taken as signaling the end of the Chicago School.

If Case had any negative feelings about the undoing of his earlier administration, these seem not to have been recorded anywhere. On the other hand, he was not above contributing an occasional revealing barb. Thus, when he heard that Sweet would be offering a summer course in 1944 at Harvard, he offered this piquant observation: "It must be that Harvard is waking up to the task of modern education. I did not suppose that it would be interested in anything so recent as American Church History."[62] Upon his graduation from the Divinity School in 1941, Sidney Mead was appointed to the Church History Department. Efforts to bring Winthrop Hudson to Chicago were relatively unsuccessful as he arrived from Colgate Rochester in

---

[59] Letter, S. J. Case, to William Warren Sweet, November 10, 1934, University of Chicago Archives, Sweet Letter File.

[60] Letter, John T. McNeill to William J. Hynes, August 17, 1970.

[61] Sweet, "Shirley Jackson Case: At Home and in His Study," 2. Sweet and Case seem to have developed a particularly strong friendship marked both by reciprocal family visits and an active personal correspondence until Case's death. For this reason, the Sweet Letter File in the University of Chicago Archives constitutes one of the best sources for Case's letters from 1930 to 1947.

[62] Letter, S. J. Case to W. W. Sweet, September 30, 1943, University of Chicago Archives, Sweet Letter File.

1945 and returned there two years later. Harold R. Willoughby's correspondence with E. J. Goodspeed during this period provides a valuable insider's
view of the demise of the historical fields at Chicago, especially the failure
to replace people in the same proportion as they departed.[63] It should also be
noted that some of these events are probably attributable to an underlying
shift in methodological preferences under the administration of Dean Bernard Loomer, that is, a move away from historically-based theological enterprises toward more philosophically-based theological enterprises.[64]

The leadership exercise by Case had significant impact not only upon
the study of Church History as a whole but also upon the study of American
religious history in particular. At Chicago, he concentrated initially upon
picking up the creative work begun by Peter Mode in his valuable *Biographical Guide and Source Book of American Church History* (1921) and
his epochmaking *The Frontier Spirit in American Christianity* (1923). Unfortunately, Mode's promising career was cut short by a marital indiscretion
which resulted in his wife's retaining Clarence Darrow and initiating di-
vorce action.[65] These events were considered of such an inherently scanda-
lous nature that Mode was dismissed forthwith from the Divinity School.[66]
Fortunately, Case was so convinced of the unquestionable need to continue
the development of the study of American religious history at Chicago that
he sought out Sweet as Mode's replacement.

Disturbed by the loss of primary sources for the writing of American religious history, Case initiated an ambitious project to seek out and collect
conscientiously such documents. By the time of his retirement, this project
had resulted in the publication of some twenty volumes under the general
title *Religion on the American Frontier*.

The systematic vigor with which Case set out to develop the study of
American religious history was, perhaps, nowhere better illustrated than in the
lengthy and detailed application which he submitted on behalf of the American Society of Church History requesting membership in the American

---

[63] See Harold R. Willoughby's correspondence with E. J. Goodspeed, University of Chicago
Archives, Goodspeed Letter File.

[64] Cf. Bernard Loomer, "The Federated Theological Faculty," *The Divinity School News* 13
(1946) 1–3.

[65] Darrow had a number of close ties to the Divinity School including friendships with both
G. B. Foster and Shailer Mathews. Until Darrow's death, he kept a bust of Foster in his study.
Darrow debated a number of Divinity School Faculty, including Case on the topic "Has Chris-
tianity Failed?" Cf. Irving Stone, *Darrow for the Defense* (New York: Doubleday & Co., 1941)
274. When the famous agnostic died in 1938, his funeral was held in the Divinity School
Chapel.

[66] Mode's prompt dismissal and his ostracism from the academic world as a whole have often
caused his name to be overlooked within scholarly litanies. Thus, Sidney Ahlstrom, for one,
assigns the credit of applying Turner's frontier thesis to American religious development to
Sweet with no mention of Mode's earlier work. Cf. Ahlstrom, "Religion in America," 320.

Council of Learned Societies in 1933.[67] Nine years earlier, he had been
elected head of the then nearly moribund ASCH. He succeeded in liberating
this professional society from what had originally been a group whose
membership and meetings had been constitutionally restricted to New York
State and elevating it to national status. Some might wish to argue as to
whether this was in fact a liberation or in reality merely the substitution of
Midwestern imperialism for its Eastern version. The immediate Presidents of
the ASCH after Case were McNeill, Sweet, and Pauck. The latter has commented that "we staged a revolution in the American Society of Church
History and we stole that organization from the Eastern Seaboard."[68]

After 1926, the society increased its membership outside the East Coast,
began having a second meeting in the Midwest each year, and began to
meet in conjunction with the American Historical Association. The society
also initiated its own review in 1932, *Church History*. Finally, ASCH undertook three major projects in close association with the Divinity School of the
University of Chicago: (a) a series of collections of American religious history documents and denominational histories, referred to above; (b) the
publication of another series entitled *Studies in Church History* which included such works as M. M. Knappens' *Two Unpublished Puritan Diaries*,
and Spinka's *A History of Christianity in the Balkans*; and (c) an attempt to
make a union card catalogue of American religious history materials held in
American libraries. This systematic attention to the development of the
resources in American religious history must be considered one of the major
accomplishments of the Chicago School in general and Shirley Jackson Case
in particular.

Upon retiring from the Divinity School in 1938, Case accepted a special
lectureship in New Testament at Bexley Hall, an Episcopal seminary in
Ohio. In 1940, he became Professor of Religion at Florida Southern College
in Lakeland, Florida, and the Dean of the Florida School of Religion. Retirement from the University of Chicago did not mark the end of Case's
scholarly productivity. In 1941, he produced his *Christianity in a Changing
World*. Two years later, he wrote his seminal work on the study of history
and historiographical method: *The Christian Philosophy of History*. This
work and the Case Festschrift, *Environmental Factors in Christian History*
(1939), may represent respectively the high-water mark of both the theoretical explication and the pragmatic application of the socio-historical method.
The Christian Philosophy of History will be treated extensively in Chapter
IV of this work. While on "retirement" in Florida, Case also found time to
found a new periodical, *Religion in the Making* (1941–1943). Unfortunately, paper shortages associated with World War II caused its early demise.

---

[67] Letter, S. J. Case to American Council of Learned Societies, May 19, 1933, University of
Chicago Archives, Mathews Letter File.

[68] Pauck, Discussion Vanderbilt Conference.

In March of 1945, while working on a substantial revision of an earlier work to be republished under the title *The Origins of Christian Supernaturalism* (1946), Case suffered a blood clot in his right leg which resulted in its amputation and his hospitalization until late May.[69] These events did not impede Case from finishing his revisions in time for a December deadline. He confided to Sweet that "the amputated leg has been a blessing in that it keeps me from wasting time running around. And I am physically in the best of health."[70] This operation did, however, mark the end of the publication of any new books or lengthy articles. Nonetheless, Case kept up his characteristic output of scholarly book reviews. In the fall of the same year, he returned to his classroom on crutches.[71] He continued this activity for the next two years until Friday, December 5, 1947, when having returned home from a full day of teaching, he suffered a cerebral hemorrhage and died.[72] He had allowed few occasions for either his fingers to "lose their cunning" or his scholarly wisdom to grow "stale and musty with disuse."

[69] Letter, S. J. Case to William Warren Sweet, June 16, 1945, University of Chicago Archives, Sweet Letter File.

[70] Letter, S. J. Case to William Warren Sweet, October 11, 1945, University of Chicago Archives, Sweet Letter File.

[71] Bowman, "Shirley Jackson Case," 12–13.

[72] Letter, Harold R. Willoughby to E. J. Goodspeed, February 5, 1948, University of Chicago Archives, Goodspeed Letter File.

III

THE SOCIO-HISTORICAL METHOD: CASE AS NEW TESTAMENT SCHOLAR

> Since the main motive for rehearsing the message of Jesus was the propagation of the new cause now sacred to his memory, it inevitably followed that the selection of material, its arrangement, and its interpretation as worked out from time to time by different preachers and authors, should ultimately portray contemporary interests quite as fully as it preserved traditional elements of genuine historical value.
>
> –Shirley Jackson Case

The next two chapters isolate as precisely as possible the socio-historical method which was envisioned by S. J. Case and the other members of the Chicago School and which figured as such a central weapon in the war against fundamentalism. Within this specific chapter, it will be seen that much of the socio-historical method originated as a type of higher New Testament criticism which accompanied Case from his work as a New Testament scholar into his subsequent work as a historian of Christianity and Christian beliefs. While some aspects or "factors" of the socio-historical method can be seen to be present in both phases of Case's career, a number of other significant factors must await his work as historian. Thus it is only within the latter phase that the socio-historical method receives its most complete explication, specifically in Case's major work, *The Christian Philosophy of History*.

Because the somewhat specialized purpose of this chapter is the location of those specific factors associated with the socio-historical method which occur in the first stage of Case's career, his work as a New Testament scholar must necessarily be treated selectively. Readers seeking a more comprehensive analysis of this area are referred to the works mentioned earlier, particularly that by Louis B. Jennings.[1]

The dimensions of the socio-historical method within this New Testament scholarship can perhaps be most directly ascertained by considering both Case's own explicit understanding and placement of this method within the history of New Testament criticism and his own use of the distinction between the historical Jesus and the Christ of faith.

---

[1] Jennings, "Shirley Jackson Case: A Study in Methodology."

Methods of New Testament Criticism

Case places the socio-historical method within the general company of recent critical historical methods which seek to understand the New Testament in a less dogmatic manner than previous approaches. Within this general group, Case distinguishes two basic types of historical methods: historical-literary criticism and historical-social criticism. The first relies primarily upon the test of literary genre; the second moves beyond this to the test of social experience.[2] The first includes *Literaturgeschichte* and very likely *Formgeschichte*. Case indicates that depending upon whether *Formgeschichte* employs a test of social experience along with the test of literary genre, it could fall into the second type of historical criticism. Otherwise, it would remain within the first type.[3] However, the socio-historical method employed by Case himself is clearly intended to be of the second type.

Historical-Literary Criticism

This approach is characterized by its focus upon the New Testament as primarily a collection of literary documents. It seeks to unravel the literary history of each document, or of the constitutive parts of composite documents, by determining their respective authors, chronologies, and most original forms.[4] Occasionally, this approach moves beyond this documentary focus by attempting to reconstruct the life history and personal religious experiences of such figures as Jesus and Paul.

For Case, any limitations found within this historical-literary method are likely to be overcome by moving beyond to the historical-social method of criticism. This does not imply that the first method of criticism is to be rejected in any sense. Case's attitude toward the two methods is one of inclusion rather than exclusion. This is to say that the second method is founded upon the concerns and practices of the first. Accordingly, Case should himself be viewed as a practitioner of both methods.

Case's practice of the historical-literary approach seems to center especially around three emphases which will continue within his practice of the historical-social approach. These emphases are "realism," "naturalism," and "literary units."[5]

---

[2] Case, *Jesus*, 103.

[3] S. J. Case, Review of Burnett Streeter's *The Four Gospels: A Study in Origins* and Erich Fascher's *Die formgeschichtliche Methode* in *Journal of Religion* 5/4 (1925) 431. The precise relationship between *Formgeschichte* and the socio-historical method will be dealt with in Chapter V of this work.

[4] Case, *Social Origins*, 22.

[5] Another implicit emphasis which could be included is the historical perspective as such. However, since this emphasis received extended explication in the second phase of Case's career, it may be best treated in Chapter IV.

Case believes that one of the keys to the earliest writings which treat Jesus in the New Testament corpus is the quality of realism. This includes such characteristics as "immediateness," "vitality," etc.[6] Accordingly, the earliest accounts of Jesus will be those which are "simpler and more lifelike in a human way"[7] and those which contain a "very lifelike picture of the genuineness of his [Jesus'] daily experience."[8] This can serve as an initial gauge to the more original accounts of Jesus:

> In the older strata of this literature the picture of Jesus is far simpler and more lifelike in a human way, while in the later strata of the literature more and more Jesus becomes the adorable Christ of Christian worship.[9]

There is a corollary to this realism in that one may "expect to find the actual religion of Jesus represented more truly by the words and deeds that are reported in connection with the scene of his [Jesus'] ordinary daily living."[10]

Further examples of this realism being used as a gauge by Case can be seen in his *The Historicity of Jesus* where it is used to accredit the historicity of the Pauline Epistles, that is, Galatians, 1 and 2 Corinthians, Romans, Philippians, and 1 Thessalonians. It is the "minute biographical details," the "personal," and "lifelike quality" of the information given in these epistles which attests to their historicity and consequently to the historicity of Jesus as well.[11] It would have been impossible to fabricate materials such as these "where definiteness and vividness of an actual situation show behind every sentence."[12] "We may at all events believe the possibility of its [a text] genuineness to be commensurate with its naturalness and durability."[13]

When faced with the categories of supernaturalism and naturalism as modes for interpretation, Case definitely opts for naturalism. This choice is most evident thematically in his *Experience with the Supernatural in Early Christian Times* (1929). Case submits that "naturalism found no room to breathe" in the three-story universe of early Jewish-Christianity.[14] However, since then insofar as the

> . . . conquest of the normal has enlarged, confidence in it has increased, and the need for the abnormal has gradually disappeared. This is no impoverishment of the spiritual possibilities of the universe, but it does mean the

---

[6] S. J. Case, "The Religion of Jesus," *American Journal of Theology* 14 (1910) 237, 241.

[7] Case, *Historicity*, 296.

[8] Case, "Religion of Jesus," 241.

[9] Case, *Historicity*, 296.

[10] S. J. Case, "Modern Belief About Jesus," *Biblical World* 37 (1911) 10–11.

[11] Case, *Historicity*, 184–85.

[12] Ibid., 189.

[13] Ibid., 231.

[14] S. J. Case, *Experience with the Supernatural in Early Christian Times* (Chicago: University of Chicago Press, 1929) 5. Later revised as *The Origins of Christian Supernaturalism* (Chicago: University of Chicago Press, 1946).

elimination of externalism, freakishness, and arbitrary intervention in the normal world order.[15]

Thus, in dealing with the interpretation of biblical literature, Case methodologically prefers natural explanations to supernatural ones. Accordingly, God should not be conceived as an external, arbitrary interventionist. The significance of Jesus should be sought in the power of his spiritual living, not in external titles or divine relationships.[16]

Case's preference for naturalism can also be seen in his exegesis of the various narratives surrounding Jesus' baptism by John the Baptist. Central to his interpretation of this event is the question of "whether the primal item in his [Jesus'] experience at this time was not his sense of new consecration to God as a spiritual father rather than a recognition of God's choice of him as a messianic son."[17] In the opinion of Case, Jesus attained his position by "placing more stress upon his choice of God than upon God's choice of him."

Although continually disavowing any role for philosophy in New Testament criticism, Case's choice of naturalism over supernaturalism as an interpretive mode would seem to imply an underlying philosophical perspective in his method.[18] In this regard, it is very interesting to note that Case is particularly fond of G. E. Lessing. Case traces his own preference for naturalism to the logic of Lessing, as can be seen in his reference to Lessing's axiom, "Zufällige Geschichtswahrheiten können der Beweis von notwendigen Vernunftwahrheiten nie werden."[19]

A third major emphasis of the historical-literary approach is the use of literary genre to assist in determining the origins of the various New Testament documents, especially the Synoptic Gospels. Case seems to have begun his career following the then basic two-document theory of B. Weiss and H. Holtzmann.[20] However, in 1912 he makes reference to the three-document theory of Burton.[21] Two years later in his *Evolution of Early Christianity*, Case seems to have moved away from any thought of "Q" as itself a

---

[15] Case, "Modern Belief About Jesus," 9.

[16] Ibid., 16–17.

[17] Case, "Religion of Jesus," 245.

[18] Case, *Historicity*, 66. In this his first work, Case classified this preference for natural over supernatural explanation as indicative of a liberal position. At the same time, he did not explicitly classify himself as a liberal.

[19] As quoted by Case in *Historicity*, 8, n. 1, "Accidental truths of history can never become the proof of necessary truths of reason," cf. G. E. Lessing, "On the Proof of the Spirit and of Power," in *Lessing's Theological Writings*, trans. Henry Chadwick (London: Adam & Charles Black, 1956) 53. See also S. J. Case, *Jesus Through the Centuries* (Chicago: University of Chicago Press, 1932) 289ff. The question of Case's philosophical preferences will be discussed at length shortly.

[20] Case, *Historicity*, 158, 213, 215, n. 1.

[21] Ibid., 215, n. 1.

document.[22] In a joint review of B. H. Streeter's *The Four Gospels: A Study of Origins*, and Erich Fascher's *Die formgeschichtliche Methode* in 1926, he calls attention to Streeter's suggestion of a four-document hypothesis.

It is in this same review that Case welcomes the advent of the *formgeschichtliche* method which attempted "to determine the historical process that gave fixity to the oral tradition as it passed into literary form, a process determined more by the use of the material in the cult life of the communities than by the literary skill of any individual authors."[23] Six months after this in his own *Jesus: A New Biography*, he seems to favor the basic approach of *Formgeschichte* by using a test of literary genres. Thus, the formation of the Gospels is compared to the stringing of individual beads, that is, traditional units of information upon a string, that is, upon a narrative theme. With regard to the Synoptic Gospels:

> They are characterized by abrupt transitions that indicate the presence of numerous blocks of traditions, like groups of beatitudes, model prayers, proverbial sayings . . . readily betraying earlier stages in the growth of gospel books. . . . These first accounts owed their origin, not to the literary impulses of outstanding authors, but to the activity of various inconspicuous disciples. . . . First orally, and then in written form, these fluid memories gradually crystalized into more formal units of tradition that ultimately were embalmed in our present gospels.[24]

The early stages in this process can be determined by "resolving the present documents into their constituent parts," that is, by unstringing the "elemental units" or beads from the string. Then one attempts to reclassify these basic units according to their own "inherent likenesses." Case himself sees some five different types of blocks of tradition: (1) those which see Jesus as a legendized hero, (2) those viewing Jesus as a didactic example, (3) sayings of Jesus "framed about an interest in the future of the Christian movement," (4) sayings of a more proverbial or aphoristic nature, and (5) admonitions cast in hortatory form.[25] Case notes that a "new school" is attempting to distinguish between earlier and later traditions, once they are so classified, by discovering "a law of evolution in the forms which a religious literature assumes in the course of its growth." In this fashion, one may attempt "to determine successive stages in the rise of tradition about Jesus."[26] In identifying this "new school" Case refers jointly to the German *formgeschichtliche* movement and to several Americans whom he considers to have predated the German movement in this task. These groups will be discussed at length in Chapter V.

---

[22] Case, *Evolution*, 360ff.
[23] Case, Review of Streeter and Fascher, 430–31.
[24] Case, *Jesus*, 97–98.
[25] Ibid., 99–100.
[26] Ibid., 101.

Historical-Social Criticism

Even if one accepts the notion of primal units of tradition as distinguishable among themselves by literary genre, it is only by reference to the historical social experiences and environmental settings that one has the "sure basis from which to assay the genuineness of its tradition" and the accuracy of its chronology.[27]

The Social Test

All other tests, such as those included under historical-literary criticism, are preparatory to the test of social experience. This social test assesses particular literary units by

> their degree of suitableness to the distinctive environment of Jesus, on the one hand, and to that of the framers of gospel tradition at one or another stage in the history of Christianity, on the other. When consistently applied, this test will prove our safest guide in recovering from the present gospel records dependable information regarding the life and the teaching of the earthly Jesus.[28]

The basic presumption of this test is that particular primal units of tradition are intimately "bound up with the life-interests of the earlier Christian society," and that their subsequent survival, selection, and arrangement into Gospel narratives is closely linked "with the evolution of the new religious movement from the days of its beginnings in Palestine down to the period of its spread over the Mediterranean world at large."[29]

It is within given contexts of particular societal and cultural settings that both the issues of Jesus' time and the issues of later Christian communities occurred. Each of these respective environments provided the background against which Christians sought to use and understand the message of Jesus.

> They [Christian preachers] hopefully sought words of his [Jesus'] relating to the organization of the community, the propriety and the methods of missionary propaganda, and every other new issue of moment. Since the main motive for rehearsing the message of Jesus was the propagation of the new cause now sacred to his memory, it inevitably followed that the selection of material, its arrangement, and its interpretation as worked out from time to time by different preachers and authors, should ultimately portray contemporary interests quite as fully as it preserved traditional elements of genuine historical value. If Jesus were to be a thoroughly efficient teacher for the people of a later day, his message had necessarily to be modernized.[30]

[27] Case, *Jesus*, 103, 109.

[28] Ibid., 113, 115.

[29] Ibid., 106–7, 109.

[30] Ibid., 407.

For Case, the test of determining the "vital social connections" of these primal units of tradition can yield basically two results. First, it can identify units or sayings which appear "vitally linked with the Palestinian society" of Jesus' time.

> Gospel traditions that dovetail normally into this experience within a Palestinian environment need not be called into question. On the other hand, when he [Jesus] is made to sponsor interest or opinions whose social appositeness emerges first in the later history of the Christian movement, one will be very hesitant about accepting the historical reliability of such data.[31]

Materials which pass this test can be used to construct a picture of Jesus. In general, Case views the social experience of Jesus and his first disciples as basically the same. This similarity of social environments when accompanied by "the vividness of the disciples' own recollections and literalness of memory" tended to lead the disciples to "paint Jesus in the main true to life." Thus, "the Gospel tradition at inception was necessarily historical."[32]

Case's approach, of course, depends directly upon the assumpton of similarity between Jesus and his immediate environment. By itself, this assumption does not provide for any distinctiveness within the person of Jesus. At this point, one could easily conclude that if any element associated with Jesus is distinct from his immediate background, then this element is not historically genuine. Anyone adhering to a high-profile Christology might wish to argue that it is precisely Jesus' distinctiveness which makes him who he is.

The second result of the social test is to isolate traditions which are of a later origin. These traditions in turn can themselves serve as a window to the particular social experience of later Christian communities up to the time of the finalizing of the Gospel narratives. So, whereas the early materials discovered by the social test are valuable for an accurate picture of the earlier history of the Christian religion, this picture of the life of later Christian communities can reveal their dominant needs and ways of appropriating the earlier words and deeds of Jesus.[33]

This still follows the assumption of similarity even though here it is applied to the correspondence between aspects of a particular Christian community and a given social and cultural setting. Thus, the previous criticism could also be applied here. Further, the process described would seem to be circular in character. Later materials in the Gospels can provide a window to the given social and cultural situations which produced them. At the same time, however, a knowledge of the chronology of social and cultural developments can provide a standard by which various Gospel materials can be shown to be later and matched with given historical situations.

---

[31] Ibid., 108, 111.

[32] Ibid., 111–12.

[33] Ibid., 105–6.

The use of the social locality in the assessment of the various literary units or traditions is what distinguishes the historical-social criticism from the historical-literary criticism. In his review of Streeter's *The Four Gospels* in 1925, Case salutes the author for moving in the right direction beyond literary criticism by appealing "to the principle of locality as a guide to the fixing of documentary sources." However, Streeter is criticized for limiting the degree of his use of the social situation:

> If the investigation had been made to include a study of the social facts in the historical experience of the new religionists, instead of restricting itself to the use of the old tools of textual and literary criticism, the conclusion reached might have been quite different and certainly would have been more valuable for the historian.[34]

This seems to be the same type of proportional critique which Case directed against the method of *Formgeschichte* as represented by Fascher's work. For Case, any defects in this method would be remedied "not by a return to the older type of literary criticism [Literaturgeschichte] but rather by more and better *Formgeschichte*."[35]

Reliance upon the test of social experience entails knowledge of the various social situations at hand during the formative period of the Gospels. This in turn creates a need for knowledge not only of biblical documents but of extrabiblical sources as well.[36] This parallels Case's historical works where a stress is placed upon the necessity of utilizing extra-literary sources. However, in both instances, this plunge into the waters of non-biblical and/or non-literary materials was not preceded by a discussion of such methodological questions as the availability, selectivity, weighing, and adequacy of such sources.

Thus, a thorough knowledge of the general history, cultures, and religions of the period involved is necessary in order to comprehend accurately the social situations within this time span. The single best example of Case's efforts toward this end can be found in *The Evolution of Early Christianity*, which will be examined in the next chapter. In this work, a thorough knowledge of classical literature, mystery religions, philosophy, Hellenism, etc., is brought to bear upon the question of influences on the development of early Christianity. This social interpretation is developed further in *The Social Origins of Christianity* (1923) and *The Social Triumph of the Ancient Church* (1933).

Functional Significance

Another consideration to which Case refers most frequently when practicing historical-social criticism, especially as accompanying the test of social

---

[34] Case, Review of Streeter and Fascher, 430–31.
[35] Ibid., 431.
[36] Case, *Jesus*, vi.

experience, is what he terms "functional significance." In time this one factor would be considered most representative of the socio-historical method.

Within the present context, Case's introduction of functional significance has the effect of redefining the question of genuine Gospel materials. Previously, the term genuine seemed coextensive with that which was "original" or "earlier." Now when used in relation to the motif of functionalism, this term is redefined in a more psychogenetic sense: "Everything was genuine insofar as it was the expression of genuine conviction and experience . . . and answered a real religious need of . . . [the] time."[37]

In similar fashion, all Christian interpreters, from the first disciples to contemporary theologians, must be evaluated "by the degree of fidelity with which they met the needs of their own time."[38]

> Every item in Christian belief at any period in history is a product of the experience and conviction of Christian people, and can be regarded as valid only so long as it serves adequately to express the sincerest convictions and deepest experiences of each new generation of Christian persons. This is the inescapable conviction to which we have been driven by the historical study of Christianity.[39]

Even Jesus himself was self-accredited by the "practical effectiveness of his conduct."[40] In this regard, Jesus' life "reveals the secret of transforming the ideal into the real."[41]

Unfortunately, Case never dispelled the existing, if unnecessary, lack of clarity which surrounds his use of the term "needs." Consequently, there is no effort to specify the locus of these needs. Are they the surrounding culture's values internalized within the Christian community? Are they indigenous to the Christian movement itself? Do they resemble the evolving pattern of needs associated with other religious movements? In like manner, there is also no clear attempt to distinguish between any levels of hierarchies of needs, as could be represented by such categories as essential versus nonessential, primary versus secondary, ultimate versus proximate, etc. Accordingly, there would seem to be no test by which needs themselves might be weighed and judged. It stands to reason that before one can assess whether a need was efficiently met, one must determine whether the need was a valid need and indeed should be met. The specific dimensions of this term, however, remain perpetually elusive throughout Case's use of the socio-historical method. In the end, this omission significantly weakened the method.

---

[37] Case, *Evolution*, 24.
[38] S. J. Case, "The New Testament Writers' Interpretation of the Old Testament," *Biblical World* 38 (1911) 102.
[39] Case, "Liberalism," 115.
[40] S. J. Case, "The Lure of Christology," *Journal of Religion* 25 (1945) 167.
[41] Case, "Religion of Jesus," 252.

In what has been discussed so far, the historical-social method of New Testament criticism has been seen to differ from the historical-literary method of criticism in two major ways; the use of the social test and the stress on functional significance. Both these differences as well as several other factors, can also be seen operating within Case's use of the distinction between the historical Jesus and the Christ of faith. All of these were subsequently carried over into the second phase of Case's career where the socio-historical method receives its fullest application.

The Jesus of History and the Christ of Faith Distinction

Central to Case's method of New Testament interpretation is his understanding of the distinction between the historical Jesus and the Christ of faith. This distinction and three subsidiary elements become central factors in the socio-historical method. Regarding Case's view of the relationship between the Jesus of history and the Christ of faith as such, it will become apparent that for him this relationship is virtually identical to that between the "essence" of Christianity and interpretations or expressions of this "essence." The three subsidiary elements are the didactic character, dynamic vitalism and non-normativity of the historical Jesus. These elements are equally central to Case's discussion of the "essence" of Christianity.

The basic attempt to make a formal distinction between the Jesus of history and the Christ of faith is traceable at least as far back as Lessing's statement in the late 1700s:

> Whether Christ was more than a man is a problem. That he was true man, if he was man at all, and that he never ceased to be man, is certain. Consequently the religion of Christ and the Christian religion are two quite different things. The former, the religion of Christ, is that religion which he as a man himself knew and practiced, which every man can have in common with him and which every man must so much the more desire to have in common with him as the character of the man Christ is made the more lofty and lovable. The latter, the Christian religion, is that religion which maintains that he was more than a man and as such even makes him the object of its worship. How both of these religions, the religion of Christ as well as the Christian religion, can exist in Christ as in one and the same person is inconceivable.[42]

Although this distinction is fundamental to Case's method of New Testament interpretation, the precise terms which Case uses in this distinction vary considerably. In 1910, Case speaks of "the religion of Jesus" and "the

---

[42] G. E. Lessing, as quoted by Case in *Centuries*, 290–91. Cf. G. E. Lessing, *Samtliche Werke* (Berlin: Lackman, 1830) 18:284. This passage is not included in Chadwick's translation mentioned earlier.

religion of believers."[43] In 1911, he distinguishes between Jesus "the historical individual" and the "heavenly Messiah."[44] The following year in his classic, *The Historicity of Jesus*, he writes of the "earthly Jesus" and the "heavenly Christ."[45] In 1914, the terms the "Jesus of history" and the "Christ of
faith" are used.[46] In 1927, Case distinguishes between "the religion of Jesus"
and "the religion about Jesus," and also between the "Jesus of history" and
the "Christ of dogma."[47] At this point, further divisions on the Christ-side of
the basic distinction are introduced, for example, "the heaven exalted
Christ," and "the pre-existent Logos."[48] In 1932, under the influence of his
move into church history a decade before, Case continues to broaden the
Christ-side of the original distinction to include some twelve types of historic
Christologies.[49]

In the first edition of *The Historicity of Jesus*, Case outlines the ways
that modern scholars attempt to relate the Jesus of history and the Christ of
faith:

> Three ways of meeting this problem have been proposed. (1) Some interpre-
> ters assert that the main content of traditional Christology finds historical
> substantiation in Jesus' earthly career. (2) Others do not think the history
> supports the traditional views, and accordingly they would construct a new
> Christology from the material brought to light by their critical study of Jesus'
> life and teaching. (3) Yet others find the connection between his historical
> personality and the religion of men today so unimportant that they eschew
> all Christological speculation and treat him as merely one of the phenom-
> ena—more or less significant—in the history of our religion.[50]

At this point in his career, none of these interpretations is adopted by Case.
He views the purpose of the distinction itself to underscore the difference
between the personal religion of the historical Jesus and all subsequent faith
pronouncements by his followers. These pronouncements tended to become a
religion about Jesus: "Out of the 'Jesus of history' enthroned in their memory
they proceeded to construct the 'Christ of faith' who became central in their
hope."[51] The chief concern of the disciples in the wake of Jesus' death was not
the religion *of* Jesus but a proper estimation *about* Jesus.[52] Thus, "Christology
is, in the last analysis, an estimate of Jesus' worth for the individual

---

[43] Case, "Religion of Jesus," 240.
[44] Case, "Modern Belief About Jesus," 10.
[45] Case, *Historicity*, 174, 296.
[46] Case, *Evolution*, 332–33.
[47] Case, *Jesus*, 339.
[48] Ibid., 2–4.
[49] Case, *Centuries*, vii.
[50] Case, *Historicity*, 309. This particular chapter is not included in the 1924 revised edition.
[51] Case, *Evolution*, 332–33.
[52] Case, *Jesus*, 328.

interpreter."[53] Not only does such a process of appraisal often tend toward the language of external relationships, official titles, and enhancing legends, but also it can cover over the religion of Jesus.

Even though Case maintains a strong distinction between the Jesus of history and the Christ of faith, he does not agree with positing a total discontinuity between the two. He maintains that "the personal religion of Jesus is the foundation of the disciples' religion about Jesus."[54] For Case, there is a definite continuity between the religion of Jesus and the Christ of faith, that is, the disciples' memory of the forceful personality of Jesus.[55]

> The impress of his personality left upon them contained an element of vitality, interpreted by them in terms of resurrection faith, which was more enduring than all their former messianic expectations, and in turn became the basis of a new messianic hope. Thus the secret of Jesus' influence upon the disciples must ultimately be sought in the content of his own personal religious life during the period of his association with them. In the last analysis it was his power as a religious individual that made possible the early faith.[56]

Therefore, Jesus' fundamental significance lies in his religious life, not in people's beliefs about him.[57] This religious life and the disciples' experience of it are prior to both doctrinal assertions and elevated significances assigned to Jesus.[58] This is to say that while the religion of Jesus is prior in logic, time, and significance to the religion about Jesus, there is still a distinct continuity between the Jesus of history and the Christ of faith.

Case is fully cognizant of the problems of attempting to identify the religion of Jesus. He acknowledges that even within early Christian literature the focus was on the religion of the believers and not on the personal religion of Jesus: "The earliest document was an apostolic product and so likely to embody some of the special tendencies of early theologizing."[59] However, at the same time such early sources, as the New Testament writings, preserved much of the personal side of Jesus' life in spite of this process of theologizing.

The Jesus of History

S. J. Case, in attempting to isolate the historical Jesus and his personal religion, finds two basic traditions within the Gospel narratives. One of these

---

[53] Case, *Historicity*, 331. For a critical analysis of Case's own attenuated Ritschlian perspective, see Chapter V.

[54] Case, "Religion of Jesus," 241.

[55] Case, *Evolution*, 334.

[56] Case, *Historicity*, 280–81.

[57] S. J. Case, "The Historicity of Jesus," *American Journal of Theology* 15 (1911) 42.

[58] S. J. Case, "Was Christianity a New Religion," *Biblical World* 31 (1908) 419, 425.

[59] Case, "Religion of Jesus," 240.

traditions depicts Jesus in a prophetic and didactic vein, and the other casts him in a more heroic light.

Heroic Figure

This tradition concentrated upon the deeds of Jesus as seen in a heroic light. Accordingly, there was a focusing upon the miraculous works of Jesus, especially his resurrection.[60] Case sees such heroic coloring in strong evidence in the Marcan picture of the religion lived by Jesus. This coloring was largely a result of the efforts of the later followers of Jesus not "to depict his own spiritual history except as the story might serve to make him seem a more worthy object of devotion."[61] Both this tradition and the prophetic-didactic tradition might theoretically have been Jewish, but "the didactic far outweighed the heroic" in appropriateness for the Judaic world.[62]

Prophetic-Didactic Figure

This tradition depicted Jesus in prophetic imagery. Consequently, Jesus was seen as one possessed by the Spirit of God. Little stress was placed upon miracles, but rather upon Jesus' prophetic activity under "the absolute imperative" of "divine impulsion."[63] Therefore, attention was directed toward the sayings of Jesus and his ideals for religious living. This stress was most evident in the non-Marcan sources in Matthew, Luke, and in the Marcan parables.[64]

The prophetic-didactic tradition is viewed by Case as earlier than the heroic tradition. He reaches this conclusion on several grounds. First, by using the social test, a ratio of appropriateness to environment can be posited. For example, a prophetic-didactic stress was seen as more typical for a Jewish situation.[65] While Case would thus characterize Jesus' historical role and work as primarily didactic, "it was not without its sense of being chosen or its heroic moments."[66] Nor was the didactic side of Judaism without strong appeal to the heroic-minded Gentile audiences. Secondly, vivid rural Palestinian imagery and Aramaic linguistic similarities in the prophetic-didactic tradition also suggest its earlier origins.[67]

However, even this earlier prophetic-didactic tradition had undergone internal revisions by the end of the first century. The didactic element, under the pressures of the organizational needs of the continuing Christian community after the failure of the immediate second coming, was increasingly

---

[60] Case, *Jesus*, 397.
[61] Ibid., 339.
[62] Ibid., 346.
[63] Ibid., 259, 343, 481.
[64] Ibid., 345, 397.
[65] Ibid., 346.
[66] Ibid., 359.
[67] Ibid., 399–406.

stylized into the exemplar of Jesus the teacher.[68] So Jesus came to be seen as the "ideal sermonizer," "the model suppliant," an authoritative teacher, and an object of worship.[69] In the light of the earliest tradition, Jesus seemingly would have repudiated the title of teacher.[70] However, to meet the needs of late first-century Christianity, "Jesus approached more nearly to the figure of the rabbi and became less and less the spontaneous prophet of reform."[71]

Case speculates that these two basic traditions, the prophetic-didactic and the heroic, may be the result of the life processes of two distinct groups of Jesus' followers. The first group, perhaps, sought to preserve the prophet's message, not unlike the followers of earlier prophets. The second group, perhaps, was concerned to declare its "new appreciation of the prophet's personality and its expectation of his early return in apocalyptic triumph." The first community might have been set within a Palestinian environment and concerned with preservation of the "things said," and lacking the experience which led the second group to religious faith.[72] The second group could have been set within a Gentile context, preoccupied with rehearsing the "things done" by Jesus; this group was destined to dominate the Gentile world with its stress on the heroic which to some extent came to include portions of the didactic aspect.[73]

The Personal Religion of Jesus

As was already pointed out, within this biographical quest it is the personal religion of the historical Jesus in particular which concerns Case. This personal religion revolves around two focal points: (1) the relation of the historical Jesus to God, and (2) the relation of Jesus to human beings.

"The outstanding feature of Jesus' religion was the prophet's characteristic awareness of the presence of God."[74] It was this "consciousness of vital fellowship with God" which forms the first focal point of the religious experience of Jesus.[75] Any unique status of supremacy attributed to Jesus arises from this oneness[76] and Jesus' loyalty to it.[77] In this fashion, one must understand Jesus not as a maker of "moral or religious credenda" or agenda, but one whose

---

[68] Ibid., 312–13.

[69] Ibid., 410–12.

[70] Ibid., 388.

[71] Ibid., 409.

[72] Ibid., 378.

[73] Ibid., 398. In these speculations, Case acknowledges the earlier suggestions of K. Lake's *The Stewardship of Faith* (1914), and E. Meyer's *Ursprung und Anfänge des Christentums* (1921). Cf. Case, *Jesus*, 396: n. 1.

[74] Case, *Jesus*, 378.

[75] Case, "Religion of Jesus," 252.

[76] Case, *Jesus*, 335. Cf. Matthew 11:25, Luke 10:21.

[77] Case, "Religion of Jesus," 252.

religion struck its roots more deeply into the life of the soul—a soul that enjoyed perpetual communion with God its Father. . . . For Jesus . . . religion was essentially an experimental affair rooted in the spiritual impulses of the inner life. Deeds were performed and words spoken out of the abundance of the heart. He who urged others to scrutinize their motives and sanctify their aspirations was himself a living example of the individual whose piety springs forth spontaneously from the depths of his being.[78]

The second focal point of the personal religion of Jesus was his sense of obligation and complete consecraton to the service of others.[79] This duty to live a life of righteousness and love for others flowed from the basal experience of God. The end of this righteous living was not to gain God's favoritism but rather the gift of one's self in God-like service to others. Therefore, Jesus himself offered no soteriological doctrine or ethics other than that individuals "became sons of God in childlike, trustful fellowship and under the inspiration of this fellowship live the life of unselfish service."[80] In his own life, Jesus preferred that his God-like life of service to humanity be his testimonial rather than any miraculous events or extravagant claims.[81]

It is Case's judgment that Christian messianism was born *ex post facto* out of (1) the dynamic impression of the historical Jesus, (2) the shock of the crucifixion, and (3) the visions of Peter and others.[82] Messianism and titles pertinent to such official self-appraisal formed no part of the personal religion of Jesus. Jesus was far more concerned with "God and the Kingdom than in creating a new messianic official." He sought to "prepare his fellow-Jews for membership in the Kingdom."[83] The Christological stimuli necessary for the development of this messianic interpretation of Jesus were historically and psychologically more appropriate to the period of the crucifixion.[84] Thus, the "historical Jesus had little in common with the heavenly Messiah except identity of personality in the mind of early Christians."[85] Any uniqueness that Jesus possessed was derived from the power with which he spoke his message, not from any official messianic status.

The Christ of Faith

Christology for Case is synonymous with theology or the process of interpretation of the historical Jesus for the needs of later times. Christology is

---

[78] Case, *Jesus*, 386–87.

[79] Ibid., 385.

[80] Case, "Religion of Jesus," 248–49.

[81] Case, *Jesus*, 262.

[82] Ibid., 375.

[83] Ibid., 377, 379.

[84] Ibid., 375–77.

[85] Case, *Evolution*, 355, 360.

the selection of particular historical data about Jesus and its speculative interpretation within the context of a particular historical Christian society with its own peculiar needs.[86] This subsequent interpretation of and elaboration upon the historical Jesus is basically a process of idealization.[87] This is due to the general need to find norms in the past for present living.[88] In particular, this process results from the attempts of Christians to "make Jesus the supreme example of whatever one imagines the ideal Christian to be in one's own area of experience and activity."[89] For Case, this process as found in Christianity was an outgrowth and continuance of *haggadic midrashim*.[90]

Case proposes a twofold norm whereby particular Christologies, or Christs of faith, or religions about Jesus could be evaluated: "Comparison with the verifiable facts about Jesus' career and an understanding of the new stimuli that from time to time inspired fresh interpretations." This dual norm in turn demands both a critical knowledge of the historical Jesus and a thorough understanding of the "successive strata of cultural developments" through which "the whole course of evolution . . . [of] interest in Jesus has passed since . . . the hopes of his expectant followers were temporarily shattered by the tragic event of Calvary."[91] With these two areas of knowledge in hand, any particular Christology can be judged as to whether it was historically accurate with respect to Jesus as well as functionally significant for its particular time.[92]

Fundamentally, each Christology is as good as another as long as it does not obscure the actual data of the life of the historical Jesus and succeeds in meeting the particular needs of the environment within which it is conceived.[93] This perspective presumes an ongoing process of Christological interpretation and reinterpretation which is both natural and necessary. Christological interpretation must be continually readjusted to the new ideas and needs of each new age. Therefore, no one Christology can ever become permanently dominant.[94]

In *Jesus Through the Centuries*, Case provides the reader with a summary of the history of Christology. Ten major Christological typologies, seven of which fall within the first hundred years of Christianity, are listed: Triumphant Martyr, New Messiah, Deified Hero, Lord of the Cult, Incarnate God, Jehovah, Jesus and Metaphysics, Jesus of Catholic Theology, Jesus

---

[86] S. J. Case, "Jesus and Historical Inquiry," *The Biblical World* 34/2 (1909) 77.

[87] Case, *Centuries*, 11.

[88] Ibid., 12.

[89] Ibid., 9.

[90] Case, "The New Testament Writer's Interpretation of the Old Testament," 95.

[91] Case, *Centuries*, 15–16.

[92] Case, "The Lure of Christology," 166. Here the social and functional tests are utilized to assess various Christologies.

[93] Case, "Modern Belief About Jesus," 14.

[94] Ibid., 7, 16.

of Medieval Piety, and the Jesus of Protestantism. A brief synopsis of these Christologies can serve further to illustrate Case's understanding and utilization of the distinction between the historical Jesus and the Christ of faith.

The initial effect of Jesus' death was not as shattering for those who viewed him in prophetic terms as it was for those who had seen him as some sort of political deliverer. The former saw Jesus' death as a semi-traditional and fitting end to his prophetic career. Subsequently, these followers viewed Jesus as the "Triumphant Martyr" and concentrated on preserving his religious attitudes and principles.[95] The Gospel of Mark exemplifies this approach.[96] Those who had seen Jesus as a political deliverer, however, found their confidence rekindled by later visionary experiences of Jesus.[97] For such a group, which included Peter, Jesus now became the "New Messiah" whose imminent return would bring spiritual deliverance. With further reflection, additional emphasis was placed upon Jesus' Davidic credentials and signs of divine approval of his mission.[98]

Increasing contact with Gentile cultures led to three other types of Christologies, each more colored by the needs and values of Gentile cultures than the last. In an atmosphere disposed to comparison with such Gentile religious models as the cult of Dionysus, Jesus became the "Deified Hero." Accordingly, stress tended to be placed upon such themes as death and revivification, as well as upon explicit comparisons with the roles played by deities and political heroes.[99] This process of deification followed a "normal evolutionary development" into another type of Christology where Jesus was the "Lord of the Cult." This typology arose out of the increasing tendency within the Christian movement to address Jesus in prayer. Constant contact with other cultures also invited the expression of Jesus' duties to include those of other honored deities.[100] Finally, this deification process reached its conclusion in the Christology of the "Incarnate God" where Jesus himself became not only an object of worship and adoration, but also a deity among human beings. The Gospel of John embodies this approach for Case.[101] This Christology was crystalized by the beginning of the second century, but not without some degree of de-emphasis and denial of the humanity of Jesus as exemplified in the rise of Docetism.[102] Gradually the genesis of the apotheosis of Jesus had been pushed back in his career until it was pretemporal, so that Jesus was identified with the pre-existent Logos of Philo.[103]

---

[95] Case, *Centuries*, 27–28.
[96] Ibid., 236.
[97] Ibid., 28.
[98] Ibid., 54–55.
[99] Ibid., 75, 81.
[100] Ibid., 85–113.
[101] Ibid., 114–15, 117–18.
[102] Ibid., 122, 236.
[103] Case, *Centuries*, 145–47.

This deification of Jesus set the theological stage for the problem of ditheism. Do Christians have two gods or do they merely have several names and titles for the same reality?[104] This problem gave birth to the Christology of "Jesus and Jehovah," with Justin as one of its leading exponents. In the resolution of this problematic area, some theologians such as Origen employed Neo-Platonic metaphysics. This in turn resulted in the Christology of "Jesus and Metaphysics." This view attempted to answer the question of ditheism by pushing the deification of Jesus back one step farther, so that the origin of the Logos was coeternal with the Father. The Son and the Father were acknowledged to share the same essence (*homousia*), but to have each a different personal entity (*hypostasis*). These logically irreconcilable positions were forcibly harmonized at Nicaea by Constantine's legal intervention, making this formula proscriptive of Catholic Orthodoxy.[105] After this, Christology became the "Jesus of Catholic Theology." This Christology is characterized by its sacrifice of logical precision to meet the needs of both imperial unity and ecclesiastical sacramentalism.[106]

Despite the later Chalcedonian affirmation of Jesus' full humanity, the "Jesus of Catholic Theology" came to be "essentially a divine and heavenly, rather than a human and earthly figure."[107] This neglect of the earthly Jesus in his humanity was offset partially by two subsequent types of Christology. The first was the "Jesus of Medieval Piety." This is visible both in examples of popular medieval piety as well as the mystical tradition of Bernard, Francis, Rudolph of Saxony, and Tauler. All of these attempted to stress a portrait of Jesus relevant to the medieval person's self-image and needs. There is an ironic twist here in that the "distinctive circumstances in Western Christianity made it the task of practical piety rather than speculative theology to preserve a lively sense of the full manhood of Christ."[108] Unfortunately, this medieval Christology was not really an attempt to return to the actual historical Jesus so much as it was a humanization of the Lord Jesus Christ of the creeds to fit medieval standards.[109]

The other type of Christology which attempted to offset the previous neglect of the earthly Jesus was the "Jesus of Protestantism." With the Reformation, Martin Luther initiated a return to the scriptures which should have led to a return to a more human and historical Jesus.

While Luther did remove many medieval excesses surrounding Jesus, he did not return directly to the historical Jesus of the scriptures but proceeded via the Christological creeds and dogmatic formulations of the early Church. Many other Protestants followed initially Luther's example; however, in

---

[104] Ibid., 178–81.
[105] Ibid., 192, 211.
[106] Ibid., 202, 209.
[107] Ibid., 243.
[108] Ibid., 247–48, 252.
[109] Case, *Centuries*, 278.

some cases, they proceeded through a second route as well, that of Protestant scholasticism.[110]

At this juncture in his work, Case's emphasis shifts from Christological typologies to the quest for the historical Jesus. Implicitly, modernity seems to be characterized by a turning from the religion about Jesus, the Christ of faith, and the production of new Christologies, and returning to a search for the religion of Jesus, the historical Jesus:

> While one might feel stimulated to chart a new course over troubled theological waters, in the hope of reaching more comfortably some familiar harbor, the possibility of finding a new continent of religious valuations could hardly be imagined. Already the Christological globe had been too frequently encircled, north and south as well as east and west. One's role was that of a canny voyager, not that of the venturesome explorer.[111]

Accordingly, Case devotes the remainder of this work, approximately three chapters, to a summary of the success and failure of this quest from the Enlightenment through the first quarter of the twentieth century.

The forte of *Jesus Through the Centuries* to this point lies in Case's ability to summarize succinctly the dynamics of that process which generates these various Christologies. However, what the book possesses in breadth it must sacrifice in depth. The format is one in which Case selects major Christological typologies and simplifies the specific details of the generative process. Particularly with respect to the philosophical background and theological implications of various Christologies, the treatment falls short of that offered by such major works as Adolf Harnack's *History of Dogma* (1884) or more recently Aloys Grillmeier's *Christ in Christian Tradition* (1965). Thus while Case treats Arius, he does not place Arianism within the process leading to the de-emphasis of the humanity of Jesus. It is commonly argued that while Arianism reversed initially the emphasis of Docetism by playing down the divinity of Jesus in favor of his humanity, the subsequent reaction against Arianism was substantially responsible for the western preference for a divine Jesus with little evidence for the humanity.[112] By the same token, in this work Case skips over medieval scholasticism and nominalism entirely, and devotes his study of medieval Christology almost totally to an exegesis of Rudolph of Saxony's *Life of Christ*.

As has already been noted, Case dates the serious quest for the historical Jesus to Lessing's assertion that "the religion of Christ and the Christian religion are two quite different things." It is with the Enlightenment that

---

[110] Ibid., 288–89.

[111] Case, *Centuries*, 312.

[112] Cf. Jean Danielou and Henri Marrou, *The First Six Hundred Years* (London: Darton, Longman & Todd, 1964) 249–67.

historical priorities override the priorities of philosophy and dogmatic theology. Previously, these sets of priorities had often been in opposition to one another. The dogmatic theologian's role was "to show how the god became a man, while for the historian the given datum was the man Jesus, and the interpreter had to explain how he became a god."[113]

Case's survey of the modern era within *Jesus Through the Centuries* takes him from Immanuel Kant and Georg Wilhelm Friedrich Hegel through Karl Barth and Emil Brunner.[114] In general, he salutes every effort to move away from the Christ of faith and towards the Jesus of history. He insists that the unassisted historical past offers religious significance in and of itself, rejecting the implicit assumption that "historical occurrences can have genuine religious worth only when estimated in the currency of some types of metaphysical and supernatural theory."[115]

It is neither historically accurate nor religiously necessary to conceive of Jesus as the pinnacle of spiritual and moral ideals, normative for all later religious living.[116] In fact, this idealization of Jesus into the norm for Christians necessitates a constant mediation between the conception of the precise dimensions of Jesus' normativity and the given religious interests of each subsequent Christian community. This results in a constant redrawing of the portrait of Jesus so as to endorse the latest religious interest and/or in a search for some inner essential similarity between Jesus' beliefs and contemporary beliefs:

> By paring down the figure of the historical Jesus to the pattern of modern religious interests, and by reducing the ideals of religious people in the twentieth century to the proper set of essential principles, a perfect equation seems to be obtained.[117]

This same syndrome can be repeated even in those who declare themselves to be in pursuit of the historical Jesus in that the interpreter can again assume that his own contemporary belief is what Jesus himself held. This syndrome can be set aside by insistence upon historical accuracy and by termination of the normative use of the Jesus of history. Historical accuracy can restrict self-serving misreadings of the details of Jesus' life; termination of normativity can remove the major motivation for attempting to collapse the past and present.

---

[113] Lessing, *Writings*, 106, 194.

[114] While the immediate concern is here limited to Case's methodological preferences, the details of this survey and a similar survey in the earlier *Evolution of Christianity*, which will be discussed shortly, can provide an interesting insight into how Case understood the recent theological past.

[115] Case, *Centuries*, 314.

[116] Ibid., 332.

[117] Ibid., 339.

Christologies should be understood as not necessarily representing "any reality beyond the sincere efforts of Jesus' ancient admirers to phrase their estimates of him in imagery and categories conformable with their social and cultural interests."[118] The religious significance of Jesus is to be found in the historical aspects of his life and religion. Jesus can function as an exemplar, but this role is neither normative nor imitative in character. Rather, Jesus can serve as an inspirational example evoking creative religious living in others.

> Creative religious living must strive not to imitate but to transcend all past and present standards, not excepting even the example and precepts of Jesus. Or more correctly stated, this type of spiritual and practical effort is not concerned with standards at all, but rather with the attainment of experiential values in the life-process as a going concern, values which when later objectivized and formulated readily become the materials out of which standards tend to become constructed. Vital contacts, which stimulate thought, awaken emotion, and contribute motive power to the personality, furnish a richer soil for the cultivation of appreciation than is possible using the category of finality.[119]

Among some of the historically accessible aspects of Jesus, which are indicative of the quality of his life, Case includes "the sincerity, the devotion, and the consecrated self-giving . . . displayed in his attempt to correct and reform religious living in Palestine," his loyalty toward both God and humanity, his moral earnestness and his confidence and zeal.[120] The significance which Jesus has for the contemporary individual is related to "the degree that we cherish and magnify in real life these elemental virtues."[121] The allowance here for "elemental virtues" is related to the issue of whether or not Christianity may be said to have an essence. This issue will be pursued in subsequent chapters.

Within this present chapter, the socio-historical method has been examined as it was envisioned and utilized initially by Case as a method of New Testament higher criticism. At least four factors have been distinguished as central to the operation of this method, particularly as taking it beyond the boundaries of the historical-literary approach: (1) the social test, (2) functional significance, (3) Case's distinction between the religion of Jesus and religion about Jesus, and (4) the character of Jesus as vitalistic, didactic, and non-normative. These same factors, joined by several others, occur in an expanded and more explicit manner in Case's work as a church historian, especially in his major work, *The Christian Philosophy of History*.

[118] Ibid., 350.
[119] Ibid., 354–55.
[120] Ibid., 367ff.
[121] Ibid., 376.

IV

THE SOCIO-HISTORICAL METHOD:
CASE AS HISTORIAN

From the point of view of historical study, life in relation to surroundings is the primal stuff out of which religions evolve. They result from man's effort to secure and perpetuate the welfare of the group or of the individual in contact with environment, particularly in its less thoroughly mastered aspects.
—Shirley Jackson Case

If the earliest, although somewhat abbreviated, expression of the socio-historical method is to be found in the initial chapters of Case's *The Evolution of Early Christianity* (1914), it is during his subsequent tenure as a historian of Christianity and Christian beliefs that this method reaches its fullest and most explicit expression in his final work, *The Christian Philosophy of History* (1943). Within this work the socio-historical method can be seen clearly at work in the treatment of two fundamental questions. What is the most appropriate perspective or world-view from which to understand the workings of history? Furthermore, how is the present to utilize the past?

To the first question, Case presents three possible answers: (1) the providential, (2) the human or (3) the dualist views of history. His preference is obviously for the human view of history which can be seen to coincide closely with the basic dimensions of the socio-historical method itself. Case's preferred answer to the second question can be anticipated from what has gone before in earlier chapters. As was true with the figure of the historical Jesus, so too the past itself should be utilized not in a normative fashion but rather in a didactic manner.

This chapter examines the more fully elaborated socio-historical method within *The Christian Philosophy of History* as it centers around these two questions. Within the method itself particular attention will be directed toward both the recurrence and expansion of previously identified factors as well as the addition of several other significant factors. Finally, the socio-historical method will be characterized by offering a comprehensive factorial profile, that is, a synthesis of those factors identified with the socio-historical method in Case's work both as a New Testament scholar and as a historian of Christianity.

The Christian Philosophy of History

If one subscribes to the conservative dictum that the title of a book should represent its contents, then *The Christian Philosophy of History* is grievously mistitled. This could be due to the publisher's wishes, as was true for Case's earlier *Jesus: A New Biography*. The phrase "Christian philosophy of history" occurs only once within the entire work.[1] Further, the term "philosophy" is itself used consistently in a somewhat negative fashion for Case, that is, as identical with "metaphysics" and as contraposed to that which is phenomenal, empirical and observable.[2] A more realistic title might have reflected the fact that this book is really more on the order of a history of the interpretation of history or a history of historiography.

In the three chapters following the introductory chapter of the book, Case identifies three major historical approaches to the doing of history: (1) the providential or sacred view of history, (2) the human or secular view of history and (3) the dualistic interpretation of history. The three remaining chapters in the book do not coincide with any other specifically identifiable historiographical approaches. However, a thorough reading shows that these last chapters are in fact a development of the theme of the second chapter, the human view of history. Thus, even though not formally acknowledged, the logical relationship of these chapters shows that the preponderance of this book deals in fact with the human or scientific view of history. This historiographical preference seems to coincide closely with Case's own socio-historical method.

This historiographical preference is also detectable in Case's intention to identify closely secular and religious history. Thus, the issue of what constitutes the most suitable method and ultimate significance of religious history is coextensive with the issue of what constitutes the most appropriate method and ultimate significance of human history. The same scientific historical method provides equal access to all historical data for both the secular historian and the religious historian. Accordingly, this method allows the secular historian to analyze the data as to its humanistic import and so to discover the secular significance of history. In addition, this same method allows the religious historian to analyze the data as to its theistic import and so to discover the religious significance of history. However, as will be noted subsequently, the secular and religious significance are in fact one and the same.

Unlike most of Case's works, the majority of this book does not appear in earlier articles. It is rather the result of his teaching and review work of the previous years.[3] However, Chapter Six, "The Religious Significance of

---

[1] S. J. Case, *The Christian Philosophy of History* (Chicago: University of Chicago Press, 1943) 216.

[2] Ibid., 57, 78.

[3] Jennings, *Biography*; see the listing of Case's book reviews in the years immediately previous to 1943, 18–24.

History," is a slightly elongated redaction of an address given in 1921 at the placing of the cornerstone of Swift Hall which would house the Divinity School.[4] For some unexplained reason, Case's treatment of twentieth-century secular and religious historians is particularly brief and many of those whom he had reviewed or commented on elsewhere are omitted.

The Providential View of History

For Case, the oldest and most continuously dominant interpretation of history in Western civilization is the providential view. An early example of this can be found in the Hebraic understanding of history. This was basically a pessimistic view in which the past was idealized and the present seen as a devolution from this past. The present was merely an interim period between a past time of divine interventionistic activity, creation and revelation and a future time of such activity, the coming of the Messiah.[5] In such a view, there tends to be a sharp distinction between secular history (the history of those outside Israel) and sacred history (the history of Israel). In addition, the Hebraic concern with the development of sacred history is not matched with an equal concern for the development of secular history.

It is this Hebraic providential view of history which the early Christians also possessed. Accordingly, for these Christians the interim of the present era was due to cease momentarily. Such an emphasis on the shortness of time sharpened the distinction between secular and sacred history for the early Christians. Thus, for Paul there was no time for making significant contributions to secular history, as exemplified in his advice to avoid the initiation or termination of all varieties of social relationships. The delay of the second coming, however, forced a moderate reorientation of this view.[6] Initially, the delay was interpreted as an opportunity to convert the Jews. However, following the destruction of the temple in A.D. 70, this delay could be utilized for the mission to the Gentiles.

The continuance of this delay into the second and third centuries, however, necessitated a more radical revison in the early Christian's view of history.[7] The providential view of history was not abandoned but widened. As the eschatological motif slackened, the church came increasingly to be seen as an enduring institution. In the wake of the Apologists' plea that

---

[4] S. J. Case, "The Historical Study of Religion," *Journal of Religion* 1 (January, 1921) 1–17. This article was republished in the Case memorial issue of *Journal of Religion* 29 (1949) 1–15.

[5] Case, *History*, 16–21.

[6] Ibid., 22–23.

[7] Ibid., 29. Apocalypticism of either an ancient or modern variety might be tied particularly to the press of historical events since it is predicated upon the occurrence of future cataclysmic events. However, as has already been indicated, given a modern version of apocalypticism during a time of war, Case was not content to let history prove such belief inaccurate. Besides, as will be noted, such a view runs directly contrary to "human activism" and the social responsibility for determining the outcome of history.

"Christians are the soul of the empire" and the subsequent acceptance of Christianity in the fourth century, there occurred a closer identification between the goals of Christianity and those of the state. To a large degree, the division between secular and sacred history was bridged. Now God's sponsorship was extended to all phases of contemporary civilization. "Christian events now became an integral part of the total historical stream. . . . Christian history was world history." This revised view of history is represented for Case in the writings of Eusebius, Julius Africanus, Jerome, Rufinus and Sulpicius Severus. Implicitly, Case identifies the providential view of history primarily with the tenet that "it is God who makes history" and secondarily, with a strong distinction between secular and sacred history. Thus, in order to have a providential view of history, it is necessary to have the first but not necessarily the second.[8]

The triumphant and confident optimism of this historical interpretation saw history as the accomplishment of God's providence through the instruments of the state and church. The fall of Rome dealt a radical blow to this confidence and occasioned a reinterpretation of the providential view of history. In the face of that, Augustine proposed returning to a split between the secular and the sacred realms of history. Augustine was pessimistic about secular history, or the history of the city of humanity, seeing it as in a process of decay. It was because Rome had become the city of humanity, that is, filled with those seeking selfish ends, that it fell. The city of God, that is, those pursuing God as their end, was viewed optimistically. Thus, sacred history promised a fortuitous outcome. It was the role of the city of God to supplant gradually the city of humanity.[9] The renewal of the distinction between secular and spiritual history was occasioned not only by Christians' horror that "the eye of the world has been put out," but also as a defense against those critics who argued with similar logic that, if God directed history as Christians claimed and if Rome had fallen after becoming Christian, then this must be God's punishment for humanity's choosing the wrong religion. Unfortunately, Augustine's inward and spiritual definition of the *civitas Dei* and the *civitas terrena* often came to have more concrete sociological referents.

In this view, the historical order was seen as providentially directed through the instrumentality of the church. This approach gives rise to later struggles between the church and state in the Middle Ages. Case sees Orosius, Salvian, Vincent of Lerins, and Otto of Freising as adopting this perspective in their writings. However, Otto's pessimistic view of the secular order terminated in an apocalypticism.[10] Ultimately, in this Augustinian providential

---

[8] Ibid., 34–41.
[9] Ibid., 48–49.
[10] Ibid., 52.

view of history "it was preeminently and eternally God who makes history" not humanity.[11]

According to Case, the providential view of history met further revision with Thomas Aquinas' application of Aristotelian categories within scholastic philosophy and theology. Here the secular and sacred were tied together in one historical process. Individuals were seen as cooperating with God in creating and redeeming. Thus, humanity is given far greater responsibility than it has in the Augustinian view since the achievement of human destiny waits upon humanity's own actions. For Case, this more optimistic providential view of history continues in the Roman Catholic church into the twentieth century as visible in the writings of such Neo-Thomists as Jacques Maritain and Christopher Dawson.[12]

In Case's mind, however, the type of providential view of history which dominates the scene up to the present time is the Augustinian view. This is largely due to its revival and repetition "without essential alteration" by the Protestant Reformation so that "the activity of God almost obliterated any human responsibility for shaping the course of providentially supervised events."[13] Case refrains from attaching the second element of the providential view, the strong separation between secular and sacred history, to the Reformation. With respect to the inadequate provision for human activity, he does not specify what particular Protestant traditions he has in mind. One could speculate as to whether Case might have been influenced at the time of the writing of this work by the then current criticisms of the seeming acquiescence of German Protestantism to the making of secular history in the Third Reich.

The Human View of History

In some ways, Case regards Thomas and later Neo-Thomists as anticipating the second major type of historiography. Thus, beginning with Thomas, running through the Renaissance and finally rising to full stature in the nineteenth century, there is what can be called the human view of history. This view of history represents a definite shift from the providential view. The human view of history manifests a greater awareness of human responsibility for making history. There is a shift in emphasis from that which is sacred, transcendent and providential to that which is secular, mundane and human.

Case's belief that Thomas anticipates the human view of history seems to be based mainly on Thomas's notion of instrumentality by which he provides for human sharing in the causality of history as a proximate agent rather than

[11] Ibid., 48.
[12] Ibid., 53–55.
[13] Ibid., 53–54.

on Thomas's positive attitude toward metaphysics. Neo-Thomists, of course, might argue that the two are not so easily divided.

This shift leads to an additional concern for locating and analyzing data and isolating and examining historical influences or causes. These two concerns were absent from the providential approach. It is because the human approach to history "shuns metaphysical speculation and worships at the shrine of empiricism" that there is a great emphasis upon the recovery of data and accurate documents.[14] These are used in attempting to reconstruct the actual historical situation. This approach might also involve the use of such other diverse disciplines as archaeology or literary criticism. Higher literary criticism is especially valuable in that it can lead one beyond the data to the tradition or situation in which the data originated as a product. The most sophisticated type of literary criticism leads one to a consideration of history in its social dimension. "The historian's search for facts embraces the entire field of man's life within his total social environment." Thus, contrary to Thomas Carlyle's dictum, history is not ultimately and merely the quest of great ones but of the "common herd of humanity as well."[15]

The human or scientific method of viewing history is deeply dedicated to isolating and analyzing the influences or causes behind historical events. Case sees this as resulting from a reaction to the nineteenth-century event-centered objectivism of Leopold von Ranke. Consequently, the human or scientific view seeks beyond events to locate the "causal nexus" or the "genetic" connection between events and their causes.[16] The chief danger in this procedure is the continual tendency toward simplification. Causal simplicity is sought by fitting "the entire course of civilization into a single hypothetical pattern."[17] This is achieved by subsuming all events as analyzable under one cause. When this occurs, the human interpretation of history becomes in fact a covert return to the providential type of historical analysis.

For Case, a Hegelian view of history can exemplify this oversimplification if it attempts to see all history as a record of the absolute idea, reason or world spirit striving to manifest itself in time:

> Thus the providential view, though in a denatured form, is once more enthroned above the processes of historical development. History is made after some prescribed pattern a comprehension of which furnishes the key to the whole.[18]

Traditionally, many have sought to find coherence in history by limiting the consideration of causes to the sole question of political motivation.

[14] Ibid., 56–57.
[15] Ibid., 63–64.
[16] Ibid., 65–66.
[17] Ibid., 132.
[18] Ibid., 68.

History is regarded as coextensive with "past politics," that is, with the story of the succession of various political leaders and their military endeavors. For Case this view, like that of Carlyle, ignores the "commonality of mankind" without which there would be no history.[19] This attempted oversimplification glosses over the fact that there is much in history which is not directly connected with politics or diplomacy and the added consideration that political events may themselves be products of the ongoing "elemental social process."[20]

Another attempt at causal simplification can be represented by the environmental analysis of history. H. T. Buckle's *History of Civilization in England* is viewed as an example of this approach. Buckle attempts to explain human cultural development on the basis of the influence of the physical environment. Lucien Febvre, H. B. George, E. Huntington and others have developed this analysis in a more sophisticated fashion in specific relation to the factors of geography and climate.

For others the role of the economic quest is the central determinative factor in the analysis of human history. Karl Marx was the most obvious advocate of this approach. In substituting rival classes of society for the Hegelian conflict of ideas, Marx did not regard history as developing toward a total manifestation of reason but rather toward an economic utopia. R. H. Tawney, Max Weber, E. R. A. Seligman and others also followed this basic analysis but with their own variant stresses.[21]

A factor which both the environmental and the economical interpretations tend to ignore is the significance of "the creative power of man's intellectual quest."

> It is very true that man cannot live without bread, but frequently he will go a long way toward denying the satisfactions of the palate in the interests of serving his appetite for intellectual, artistic, moral, and social ideals.[22]

An equally significant factor, also often ignored by these attempts at oversimplification, is the religious quest with its adherence to spiritual ideals. It is also noteworthy that the significance of the intellectual and religious creativity of humanity is here defended. Case explicitly rejects what some see as the major failure of the socio-historical method—that it tends toward external environmental determinism to the neglect of the dynamic human dimension.[23] Although Case is critical of such overtly simplistic determinism, his own failure to reflect on the internal processes whereby ideas grow and

[19] Ibid., 129–30.

[20] Ibid., 69.

[21] Ibid., 70–72.

[22] Ibid., 73, 75.

[23] Cf. E. F. Scott, "A Social Interpretation of Early Christianity," *Journal of Religion* 4 (1924) 320–21. Also see John Knox, "Memories."

develop leaves the reader by default with the impression of external determinism. Such an omission must be regarded as a major flaw in Case's socio-historical method.

Interpretations of history which attempt to subsume all data under a single category are guilty of causal simplicity. Implicitly, if not explicitly, such attempts deny the causal complexity and "multitudinous forces" which are at work in history. If one honestly faces the limitless complexity of history, then numerous causal factors must be acknowledged. In fact, "no single cause can be set above all others."[24]

> In order to understand the past, we must recognize that history is constantly on the move. It is a continuous product of human living by a great multitude of different persons in widely varied settings and under the impulsions of diverse interests.[25]

Accordingly, the most accurate human or scientific view of history will stress its complexity and hesitate to represent it in a simplified fashion.

In addition to its concern for the collection of empirical data and the causal analysis of historical events, the human or scientific view of history is deeply concerned with the question of terrestrial progress. This concern is antithetical to the providential view which regards human history as simply regressive.

The problem of historical progress may be approached from either a "philosophical" or an "observational" perspective. The former perspective seeks to locate an inescapable metaphysical principle of progression or an "inevitable law of development that insures advance despite all the shortcomings of individuals."[26] Case refers his readers to more extensive treatments of this perspective as found in E. Troeltsch's *Der Historismus und seine Probleme* (1922) and J. B. Bury's *The Idea of Progress: An Inquiry Into Its Origin and Growth* (1921).

Having selected a principle, such as that the betterment of society will result from humanity's personal moral or intellectual growth,[27] or a natural law, such as the struggle for the survival of the fittest, one then argues from this principle to its historical manifestations. At this point, the philosophical attempt to estimate historical progress seems to coincide with Case's view of attempts to estimate historical causality under the genus of a single category.

The observational approach adopts an empirical stance. Therefore, there is no initial interest in either metaphysics or natural law. On the contrary,

---

[24] Case, *History*, 76, 126.

[25] Ibid., 133. As will be indicated momentarily, within the midst of this infinite variety Case can find a "perpetual continuity."

[26] Ibid., 78.

[27] Ibid., 150. This is viewed as the naive position of Diodorus and Plutarch, that is, that knowledge of good will lead to its pursuit.

history is investigated for concrete instances of progress. Initially, the observer is impressed with the tremendous flux within history. Even norms themselves seem subject to change. In terms of fixity, "nothing stays permanently put in the constantly moving current of historical evolution." Consequently, in testing for progress it is necessary to realize that the norms for progress may themselves evolve. "Progress is in [the] process of becoming; it has yet to arrive at any final goal."[28]

Case maintains that when the observational perspective considers the totality of human history, it could establish evidence of progress in the areas of material well being, intellectual knowledge, technical skills and inventions. However, progress in the areas of social, political and spiritual life is less immediately evident. Any attempt to estimate progress in the social area is made exceedingly complex because each new achievement in this area is coincidental with the discovery of new needs for future achievement. Still, when viewed realistically, "no other area of civilization will exhibit clearer evidence of progress" because "society for the common man today exhibits amenities and opportunities such as he has never before been privileged to enjoy."[29] Although Case's assessment of the historical process is guarded, progress remains fundamentally less ambiguous than it did for his contemporary Reinhold Niebuhr: "The 'laws' and tendencies of historical development proved in the light of contemporary experience to be much more complex than any one had supposed. Every new freedom represented a new peril as well as a new promise."[30]

Progress in the political area is far more uncertain. This area lags behind all others in that people have still not learned to live together without violence and war. Yet, the present keen awareness of this may in itself be a sign of progress. In the aesthetical, moral and spiritual areas there have been definite landmarks of progress in the past. Still this should not mean that progress in these areas is denied to the present age. "Never before have so many men been capable of aesthetic appreciation, moral idealism, and spiritual striving." This restless impulse toward higher achievements is more dominant than ever before, and in this lies "the surest guaranty of progress."[31] This strong element of progressivism in the writings of Case and his Chicago colleagues has understandably led to the suggestion that their modernism should be viewed as a religious version of the general social progressivism so strong in America during the same period.[32]

---

[28] Ibid., 80–81.

[29] Ibid., 84.

[30] Reinhold Niebuhr, *Faith and History: A Comparison of Christian and Modern Views of History* (New York: Charles Scribner's Sons, 1949) 7.

[31] Ibid., 84–86.

[32] For a recent example of such an analysis, see Stephen H. Wuster, "The 'Modernism' of Shailer Mathews: A Study in American Religious Progressivism, 1894–1924" (Ph.D. dissertation, University of Iowa, 1972).

A further concern of the human or scientific view of history is the effort to find some overall meaning within the historical process. The previous distinction between the metaphysical perspective and the observational perspective is seen by Case as also applicable to this issue. Accordingly, there are some who seek to give history meaning by means of a single hypothesis which is really external to the historical process. This may be the Aristotelian unmoved mover, blind fate, the Hegelian absolute spirit, a natural law, etc. In fact, however, this approach succeeds only in stretching historical events "upon the Procrustean bed of some extratemporal hypothesis."[33] Of course, for Case this seems to be but another instance of the fallacy of introducing metaphysics into history.

The observational approach attempts to locate the meaning of history within the historical process itself and does not allow the limits of experimental knowledge to be transcended. This approach, however, is itself divided into those favoring an atomistic analysis and those favoring a more totalistic analysis. The first seeks guidance for the present from particular isolated events in the past.[34] The second seeks to comprehend the nature and significance of the continuity of the historical process as holistic. In turn, this second group is subdivided into optimistic and pessimistic interpretations.

For Case, the pessimistic observational interpretation of the meaning of history is a recurrent point of view. It has found expression in Jerome's belief that the eye of the world was put out with the fall of Rome, in the Duke of Wellington's deathbed thankfulness for death lest he be forced to witness the fall of civilization and in Oswald Spengler's view that time had run out for humanity.[35]

As one might have anticipated from Case's strong attack on a pessimistic interpretation of history in his early *The Millennial Hope* (1918), the observational approach is viewed as terminating necessarily in an optimistic interpretation of the meaning of history. Over and against all pessimistic prophecies of doom,

> history goes on being made. At every turn it exhibits *a strange recuperative power* that ultimately negates every mood of discouragement and fear. . . . We must concede to history *a vitality* that refuses to bow before the decrees of our most ardent pessimists. . . . No germ of disease has ever yet shown itself so deadly that it could utterly annihilate history or prevent successive rebirths of cultural development. *It is in this mysterious fact that one seeks the ultimate meaning of history.*[36]

---

[33] Case, *History*, 148.
[34] Ibid., 149–50.
[35] Ibid., 132, 152–53.
[36] Ibid., 153–54. Italics added for emphasis.

The human or scientific view of history, with which Case most closely identifies his own position, accounts for this mysterious enduring power and vitality by regarding history as a complex product of both material entities—which viewed on the analogy of physical nature are seemingly inevitable and stable in procedure—and human beings who offer history a spiritual element which endures although it is often unpredictable and variable:

> It is *this spiritual freedom of man*—his pursuit of choice, the exercise of his will, the determinative effect of his decisions, his susceptibility to ideals, his response to envisaged values, his feeling of communion with unseen forces, his yearning for larger knowledge, his restless quest for new experiences—that *constitutes his chief significance for the making of human history.*[37]

The interplay between the material and spiritual elements of life gives history "its ultimate significance. This we may call 'the religious meaning' of the past."[38] Thus, for the human or scientific view of history, and for Case, the mysterious vitality of history which gives history its ultimate significance is attributed mainly to the spiritual freedom of human beings. Further, this overall significance of history from the scientific view is coextensive with the religious significance of history.

Historical Dualism

The third major type of historiography is a twentieth-century phenomenon formed in large part as a reaction to the pervasiveness of historical thinking in the nineteenth and early twentieth centuries. In fact, this reactionary type of historiography is really a revival of the historical dualism implicit in the providential view of history. This historical dualism rejects both the previous stress on the continuity of history and the attempt to view the historical process in developmental and progressive terms. In the place of the "unifying hypothesis of progressive historical development" there are irreconcilable contradictions now established.[39] Søren Kierkegaard's philosophy of crisis and Karl Barth's dialectical method are the foremost representatives of this historical dualism.

In posing such a sharp contrast between the imperfection of human beings and the absolute righteousness of God, this approach seems to counsel complete terrestrial pessimism as the key to celestial optimism. "This Christian philosophy of despair consigned history to the cosmic rubbish heap."[40]

God is placed above normal historical processes and a human being's access to God is greatly limited. Therefore, Kierkegaard regards God as a transcendent absolute but denies the Hegelian access to this absolute through

---

[37] Ibid., 155–56. Italics added for emphasis.
[38] Ibid., 156.
[39] Ibid., 93.
[40] Ibid., 96.

the process of gradual expressions and realizations in time and space. For Karl Barth, the notion of God as immanent in the mundane world is rejected as are the possible roads of access through the "orderly processes of nature," "the rational operations of the human mind," and even in the "moral idealism of mankind." Time and eternity, humanity and divinity, secular and sacred history are all seen as functioning in two distinct and even, perhaps, antagonistic orbits.[41] Religion is relegated to the realm of the suprahistorical:

> Religion is no longer envisaged as a human attainment in man's struggle to apprehend and perform the divine will. Rather, it is a donation from the outer world of eternity, a supernaturally mediated revelation, that has impinged upon the temporal world. Men accomplish their salvation by passively accepting the divine decrees, not by growing in historical righteousness. The underlying postulates of this type of thinking allow no place for the self-revelation of God in the area of human experience, nor is his kingdom to be realized by any progress in historical evolution.[42]

While Case admits that the views of Kierkegaard and Barth were suited to both of their own historical situations, he is critical of Barth's stress upon the helplessness and depravity of people because it could result in a decline in concern for human participation in the process of history. Without entering the debate about Barth's view of ethics or social action, it should be noted that this criticism implies that for Case there may be concerns or structures which transcend just the functional meeting of needs in given situations. Of course, it could have been argued that such human involvement in history was an ongoing "need" of humanity and society.

There have been less radical forms of this dialectical dualism. Case notes the examples of Nicolas Berdyaev, Paul Tillich and Otto Piper. They, in contrast to Kierkegaard and Barth, try to deal explicitly with an analysis of history. All three tend to separate history into two spheres, yet they all make room for the doctrine of human freedom. Like their more radical cohorts, these thinkers reflect in their dualistic views the influence of their own historical environments. Berdyaev, according to Case, views temporal history as the story of conflict and tragedy. With the coming of Christ, a new meaning was given to tragedy and suffering for they were then revealed as existing in the heart of God. After this, we are presented with a choice of two types of tragedy, human or metaphysical. If we choose the latter, we may conquer tragedy, but this victory is reserved to a trans-historical eschaton.[43] Tillich is seen as analyzing temporal history as an interaction between the conditioned and the "Unconditioned." Human freedom consists of struggling

---

[41] Ibid., 98–101.
[42] Ibid., 98.
[43] Ibid., 102–4.

to overcome the demonic in this world by faith in the Unconditioned. However, this struggle can never be consummated temporally but only beyond time. Piper offers a return to Augustine's providential view of history. Secular history or the improvement of the world order is not the concern of the Christian. The individual Christian is to be totally God-directed, seeing religious history in millennial terms.[44]

Case enumerates several other milder forms of historical dualism. Gerald Heard is regarded as offering an analysis of history as a dualistic struggle between the war mania as a frustration arising from the unsuccessful attempt to achieve a world order consciously and the necessity for the world to be governed by people's subconscious. John Macmurray stresses the view that it is the separation between rational thinking and practical activity which is at the root of present events. Here Christianity is regarded as valuable because it exemplifies the "continuity of an intention incorporated in practice." Accordingly, Christianity forges a unity between thought and practice and initiates a new type of history. Finally, C. H. Dodd is seen by Case as also accepting this historical dualism with its consequent depreciation of secular history.[45]

Ultimately, Case sees the historical dualist as opting for a metaphysical rather than an observational view of history:

> Either a hypothetically determined meaning is read into historical incidents or else they are denied the very possibility of meaning. It has to be superimposed from without—if, indeed, it is not an absolute reversal of those values that inhere in observable historical phenomena.[46]

This view looks beyond the meaning of the actual events to "the secrets of the superearthly history" to give temporal history its meaning. Unfortunately, that opens an avenue for escape from the harsh realities of recent secular history. While this view has rightfully refocused attention on the real presence of evil in the wake of a more optimistic age, the unfortunate price for this is the dividing of history into two realms, the releasing of humanity from responsibility for secular history, and the separating of the immanence of God's sustaining parenthood from human strivings.[47]

Case's argument is that the meaning or significance of history must come from within and not be imposed arbitrarily from without, especially in a way which separates history into secular and sacred. Nonetheless, this language often leaves a nominalist aftertaste. One might wish that Case had defended on a theoretical level the necessity of abstractions and generalizations in the writing of history as vigorously as he utilized the same in

[44] Ibid., 104–9.
[45] Ibid., 110–17.
[46] Ibid., 118.
[47] Case, *History*, 122–23.

practice. After all, as G. R. Elton has so aptly put it: "Meaningful interconnection in the particular, illuminating generalizations beyond the individual case—these are the marks that distinguish the inspired and inspiring historian from the hack."[48]

The Uses of History

A dominant theme to which Case returns persistently in various writings is the use of history. Central to this concern is his distinction between the use of history as normative and the use of history as didactic. This distinction is used to deal with both the secular meaning or use of history and the religious meaning or use of history. The employment of this distinction equally in both areas points up again the essential similarity in method and significance between secular history and religious history for Case. As already mentioned, this underlying unity is evident also in the fact that Case's own methodology is the same whether concerned with the secular meaning of the past or with the religious meaning of the past.

The Normative Use

The normative use of history is often a practical attempt to authenticate some present structure or idea by reference to a past period in history. This can be simply a result of apathy toward change in the present: "The rank and file of humanity do not want to be the first by whom the new is tried, and they are often quite content to be counted among the last by whom the old is set aside."[49] On the other hand, the normative use can result from an idealization of the past as golden and a view of the present as merely a deteriorization from this past.[50] This notion of the normativeness of certain past periods can be seen in the use of classical standards in art and music, in the believed normativeness of initial constitutional documents for particular nations, and in the supposed normativeness of revelation, creeds, and doctrines for religions.[51] Thus, in the normative view, past models tend to become criteria for present options.

In Case's mind, even recent secular historians and the "new church historians" while attempting to use scientific procedures in their work often still have "retained enough of their a priori values to leave in their works a large place for the normative character of the Past."[52] F. C. Baur's investigation of early Christianity "proved it to be a religion of moral universality of exactly the type needed in his own day." This is true to some extent also in all the

---

[48] G. R. Elton, *The Practice of History* (London: Collins-Fontana, 1967) 126.

[49] Ibid., 145.

[50] Case, "Historical Study of Religion," 14.

[51] Case, *History*, 138–40.

[52] S. J. Case, "The Rehabilitation of Church History in Ministerial Education," *Journal of Religion* 4 (1924) 233.

leading rekindlers of historical study in the nineteenth century such as Henke, Gieseler, F. C. Baur (who represented a liberal position), Neander (who represented a conservative position), and the Ritschlians, including Harnack (who represented a position of mediation).[53] The traces of the normative use of history can be seen in the United States' own Neander, Phillip Schaff. Case views Schaff's *History of the Christian Church* as representing the high-water mark for this combination of scientific method and normative value in the doing of history:

> [This work represents] the most substantial piece of work in the field of church history that has been produced upon American soil. But instead of its marking the beginning of an awakening interest in the subject among American theological students, as the author has optimistically viewed the prospect, it might be truly said to represent the last ripple of the receding wave which had swept across from Germany in earlier years. At any rate, one must admit that church history has not been a subject of growing vital interest to students in American theological schools since the early nineties of the last century.[54]

For Case, this decline in the normative use of history results mainly from the influence of scientific thought itself as well as from the misuse of the normative approach. In addition, the ideality of the past is undermined by the modern dynamic and evolving view of the universe. "The youth of the world is found to have been a period of simple beginnings rather than an age of slightly tarnished perfection but a short step removed from its supposed divine prototype."[55] Also, the newly discovered massive length of history vies against ascribing ideality to its beginnings:

> . . . when the modern scientist affirms without a tremor of a doubt that human history began a quarter of a million years or more ago, the past becomes so unwieldly that it gets out of hand, and even the most unrestrained theorist would hardly venture nowadays to ascribe the character of ideality to those remote beginnings of the human career. The Golden Age of antiquity, once supposed to have been a period of paradisaic perfection for man, now evaporates in a mist of mythical fancy.[56]

Accordingly, when history is viewed scientifically and seen as an evolutionary process, no earlier age can remain authoritative for a later age. Further, because past and present are more clearly differentiated, supposed normative

---

[53] Ibid., 227, 233.

[54] Ibid., 230. The last portion of this statement may reflect the realities confronting Case in the previous year since he had become chairman of the Church History Department.

[55] S. J. Case, "The Religious Meaning of the Past," *Journal of Religion* 4 (November, 1924) 579. Cf. Case, *History*, 212.

[56] Case, "Religious Meaning of the Past," 579.

models from the past are not so easily or summarily transplanted into the present.[57]

Scientific thought also helps to undermine the supposed infallibility of various historical sources. Case sees this as especially true of biblical literature under the impact of lower criticism in the 1880s and 1890s.[58] Because of this undermining, these historical sources lose their normative character. Yet at the same time, the scientific milieu encourages the search for accurate documents and historical data. This effort results in the documentary method of historical analysis. Unfortunately, the initial effect of this method when linked with the decline in the normative value of the past is that documents were increasingly deprived of life. They are seen as dead entities and as storehouses of objective facts of doctrines. Case sees B. J. Kidd's *A History of the Christian Church to 461 A.D.* (1922) as an example of this approach.[59]

Higher criticism, as it was referred to then, pushes beyond the documentary method by considering the genesis of each document. One instance of this criticism was linked with a specific group's reaction against the supposedly "objective" approach to the documents. This group saw itself as writing "a new history" which would "make society rather than documents their point of departure in reconstructing the story of the past." "The ultimate unit in history is not the document but the contemporary social order of which the document may have been merely an incidental product."[60] While Case does not explicitly identify the members of this group, it seems clear that he intended to include in a primary manner the users of the socio-historical method.

Within this group, documents are understood and utilized as reference points to the vital social process which originally produced them. When this is done, documents are neither normative nor dead, but didactic and living. When documents and institutions are viewed as products of the social process, they provide the historian with a "whole set of new values." This approach offers the opportunity of isolating the experience behind these historical products and this in turn necessitates the rewriting of history in the light of "social phenomena."[61] This concern for the social process behind the documents is an expansion of the "social test" which was seen earlier in Case's career as a New Testament scholar. E. C. Colwell believes that even Goodspeed, the eminent documentarist, was influenced by this social approach as evidenced in his *New Solutions to New Testament Problems* (1927).[62]

<hr>

[57] Case, "Historical Study of Religion," 3, 14.
[58] Case, "Rehabilitation of Church History," 232.
[59] Ibid., 241–42.
[60] Case, "Historical Study of Religion," 4.
[61] Case, "Rehabilitation of Church History," 239, 242.
[62] Colwell, "Chicago School," 17. Cf. Knox, "Memories," 26.

The Didactic Use

The major alternate use of history for both the secular and the religious historian is the didactic use of history. Even though the impact of scientific thinking has caused the decline of the normative use of the past, this does not mean that the study of the past is useless. The past can be both a valuable wellspring from which one may draw and a significant horizon against which one may stand. In short, the past can serve the present without necessitating the regulation of present beliefs or actions according to past norms.

The didactic approach can deepen people's appreciation of the continuity between the past and the present. Accordingly, it can reveal both the modernity of ancient humanity and the antiquity of modern humanity. It can also show the extent to which human concerns have or have not been similar or consistent throughout history. Unlike the normative approach, the didactic approach does not have to presume total or essential similarity between a past period and the present since it is not necessary to make aspects of the past normative for the present.[63]

Nonetheless, solutions from the past can still be used in the present when they demonstrate themselves relevant to present needs: "The perpetuation of heritages from the past will derive justification solely from the measure of their functional value in the experiences of the continuing Christian society."[64]

Against this acknowledged background of continuity and similarity, the didactic approach to history can exercise a correlate role in pointing up the novelty and dissimilarity of the present with the past. The advent of mechanization and industrialization, for example, creates new types of opportunities as well as social problems. The radical discoveries in scientific and historical knowledge themselves create a new understanding of the world, time, and humanity. Accordingly, the didactic role of history is able to show that while the present "is partially a replica of the past, it is also a distinctly new thing under the sun."[65]

In identifying vestiges of the past in the present, the didactic method may also often show how and why a particular reality came to be significant in the past and preserved into the present. This is accomplished by attempting to set out the conditions under which this reality was "functionally significant." It can then be estimated as to whether this reality was preserved in a later period because it continued to be functionally significant or because it had become enshrined in the traditions of "conservative impedimenta." For the modern, this knowledge of the processes of historical evolution, gained by the didactic view of history, is alone that which "can make one intelligently at

---

[63] Case, *History*, 137–40.
[64] Case, "Religious Meaning of the Past," 587.
[65] Case, *History*, 141–43.

home in this inescapable world."[66] Confronted with the decision to preserve
or eliminate a particular tradition, one can make a decision on the same basis
as that on which the tradition was created, that is, functional significance.

This implies a further use of the didactic use of history for Case—the
revealing of the true significance of possible options in the present.[67] This
involves the identification of present options as new or as models from the
past. In regard to the latter, a model which has been generally successful in
the past is to be preferred to one which has been unsuccessful:

> The probable outcome of a particular line of action may be foreseen in the
> light of a given set of antecedents and consequents that have often repeated
> themselves in the past. Procedures that have repeatedly proved futile in the
> course of history may be avoided under the guidance of better knowledge.[68]

However, it is not sufficient to examine the past success or failure of a particular past model to understand its true significance as a present option.
Otherwise, this would be the normative use with its implicit assumption that
anything which worked in the past will work in the present. Rather, it is
necessary to understand the vital social situation within which this past model was successful by being functionally significant. At the same time it is also
necessary to understand the present vital social situation. Then it can be
judged better whether the particular past model can offer functional significance as an option in the present. New models which have no historical
precedence must be evaluated solely in terms of their supposed functional
significance for the present.

The didactic use of history also enables the user to distinguish between
a particular movement as a social phenomenon and its various by-products,
such as institutional structures, ideas and doctrines. The didactic presentation of this underlying social vitality can be educationally transformative in
the present, in that "we meet new people, share their life in other environments, and increase our capacity for understanding and pursuing the business of life today."[69] The didactic approach offers a similar result for the
historian specifically concerned with the religious significance of history.
Therefore, the didactic use of history can be "a means of restoring, as far as
possible the total range of Christian experience, both of the individual and
of the group, realized with the Christian's own society and in relation to
their environment."[70]

The final, and perhaps the most important, value of the didactic use of
history is that it can demonstrate the crucial role of human responsibility in

---

[66] Ibid., 88–89.

[67] Case, "Rehabilitation of Church History," 238.

[68] Case, *History*, 89, 144.

[69] Ibid., 88.

[70] Case, "Rehabilitation of Church History," 242.

the ongoing process of history. All past cultures, ideas and societies are seen as products of the human exercise of creative responsibility. Accordingly, all future progress is seen as inherently dependent upon a person's exercising responsibility, that is, being engaged fully in a strenuous activism.

> Perhaps the outstanding value of history, when viewed as the long record of human activity, is a new sense of man's responsibility for creating a better society. Man makes his own world of culture; civilizaton is the product of his ideals and activities. . . . In no sphere of culture will man's attainment rise above the level of his most strenuous endeavors. . . . The human view of history seeks to portray the story of the past as a vital process of man's endeavor in every area of his activity. . . . Strenuous activism is held up to view as the only program that will insure success. The future will be exactly what men make of it, whether they strive merely in their own strength or seek divine guidance for their endeavors. In either event the full responsibility rests with them.[71]

"Each generation is the creator of its own changing culture. The world of today will be good or bad in proportion to the creative energy displayed by man throughout the vast areas of activity over which he exercises control."[72] The didactic use of history points up this same fundamental responsibility in regard to the religious significance of history:

> Each generation of Christians, although rightful heir to all that had gone before, has also been genuinely the maker of the specific Christianity of its own age. . . . In the presence of new persons, new environments, new experiences, and new knowledge, a new Christianity is always in process of becoming, and no small measure of responsibility for directing its course rests on the shoulders of its duly appointed leaders.[73]

These last remarks form a part of an address delivered by Case at the opening exercises of the Divinity School in October 1924. In this same address, he utters what might be regarded as an apt epigrammatical summary of the didactic use of history: "The past is yours in so far as it serves your needs, but you are never its servants."[74] Of course, at this point the didactic and functional approaches to history are virtually coextensive.

The Didactic Use of History in Theological Curricula

As previously shown, Case conceives of the swing from the normative use of history to the didactic use of history as paralleling in general the acceptance of scientific methods and insights by historians. This is true both

---

[71] Case, *History*, 89–91.
[72] Ibid., 147.
[73] Case, "Religious Significance of the Past," 589.
[74] Ibid., 591.

of those historians seeking the human significance of history and many of
those historians seeking the religious significance of history. In his role as
chairman of the Church History Department and later as Dean of the Divinity School, Case sees several unique problems arising when this change
from the normative to the didactic use of history takes place within a theological curriculum which in large part was designed for students aiming at
the ministry.

In the early 1920s, he sees these problems as manifested in a lack of
interest in the study of history within the theological curriculum. He traces
this phenomenon to several factors: (1) the decline of the normative value of
history, (2) the pervasiveness of a general historical perspective which
seemed to make specific historical studies unnecessary, (3) a reluctance to
transcend the documentary method, and (4) a new interest in the social sciences.

The decline of the normative use of history, owing to causes previously
outlined, seems initially quite disastrous for a curriculum designed largely
for the practical ministry. With the decline of the normative use of the past,
church history seems to lose its "functional significance for the new generation of ministerial student."[75] Previously, the normative or supernaturalistic
view of history was able to furnish the future minister with exemplars and
norms for guidance. Such a person "trained his searchlights upon the past in
order to discover thereby the character of the divine decrees that authenticated his chosen institution or validated his particular type of doctrine."[76]

The initial result of the impact of scientific method upon the study of
church history is the documentary method. Careful collection of accurate
documents, a "more rigorous restraint of the imagination" in accord with
lower criticism, and a search into the literary genesis of the materials in
accord with higher criticism became the order of the day.[77] Unfortunately,
the more scientific church history becomes, the less valuable it seems to be
for the student:

> In becoming scientific, church history seemed to have become barren, or at
> least fallow. The more its soil was furrowed by the processes of criticism the
> less it seemed to promise in the way of a harvest of practical values for min-
> isterial education. . . . Documentary emphasis in historical study has met the
> needs of no large class of ministry students. . . . He who pursues his educa-
> tion for the ministry with a view to equipping himself with a quantity of
> normative information about the institutions or dogmas of Christianity finds
> this method of instruction very unsatisfactory. *The more critical his histori-
> cal investigation, the less in quantity is the desired yield of his labors.*
> When he learns that apostolic authority cannot be attached to the Fourth

---

[75] Case, "Rehabilitation of Church History," 230.
[76] Ibid., 231.
[77] Ibid., 232.

Gospel, that the letters of Timothy and Titus do not carry the authority of Paul, or that Constantine's marvelous conversion in connection with the Battle of Milvian Bridge is not to be credited, the student is thereby losing a number of old and well-tried weapons for the authoritarian presentation of Christian history.[78]

Case is not surprised that this decline in the normative value of the past, as well as the study of church history itself, occurs during the two decades of the twentieth century when there is such an emphasis on the historical character of theology. "Historical criticism, historical method, historical theology, historical biblical study, historical mindedness, and the like are familiar slogans in our modern theological vocabulary."[79] This is a period at Chicago when theology is synonymous with historical theology. In 1905, Shailer Mathews remarks that "every theologian must be a historian."[80] In 1924, however, Case seems to conclude that this perspective had resulted mainly in slogans rather than in actual serious study of the entire Christian past.[81]

As was stated earlier, the two decades following Case's appointment as chairman of the Church History Department were the occasion for the reversal of this trend and came to represent the beginning of this department's greatest era. In this way, Case's reflections in October 1924, represent a prospectus of the attitudes which would underlie his actions in the next decades. In short, he provides substance to what may have been to date more slogan than reality.

The fourth reason for the decline of interest in church history results directly from the previous three reasons. Deprived of normative guidance from the study of history, many students turned to various social sciences, such as sociology, psychology and education. Early in the twentieth century these disciplines were introduced into the theological curriculum at Chicago, where they were greeted not only with enthusiasm but also occasionally with the attitude that "the present and the future seemed to be sufficient unto themselves."[82]

At the same time, however, Case is heartened that this initial enthusiasm for the social sciences as sole mediator to the needs of the present seems to be waning and a "new and healthful stage of development" appeared evident. Individuals in these fields had approached Case with the observation that they felt the need for a better historical background. These individuals now wanted

---

[78] Ibid., 233–35. Italics added for emphasis.

[79] Ibid., 226.

[80] Shailer Mathews, *The Messianic Hope in the New Testament* (Chicago: University of Chicago Press, 1905) 320.

[81] Case, "Rehabilitation of Church History," 226.

[82] Ibid., 237.

to give their research "a longer perspective and a more substantial content."[83] For Case, this confirms his belief that these sociological and other contemporary issues are inseparable from history. Both humanity and society, the two central interests of the sociological discipline, are deeply rooted in the past. Theologians or ministers trained in these social sciences but unacquainted with history may very well be confronted with historical elements in modern Christianity which they cannot understand. Furthermore the same persons may also be ignorant of the variety of options for achieving good which the past has revealed.

> If the modern minister would understand his task of leading present-day Christianity out along the line of greater efficiency in modern society, he will do well to supplement his surface observations of present-day social phenomena by turning to the social history of Christianity as a whole.[84]

In the end, however, some issue must be taken with Case's preference for the didactic use of history over the normative use. One must wonder aloud whether or not normativity is all that easily avoided. Could it not be argued that Case's own didactic use of the past here seems to take on an aspect of normativity? Thus, is he not merely inverting the common sequence of the normative process whereby the present is subjugated to the past so that now the present seems to exercise a type of normativity over the past? If this is so, then perhaps the historicism of the present is merely being substituted for the historicism of the past.

Religion as the Proper Object of Historical Study

Just as contemporary religion for Case has the definite need to admit the historical and social perspective in continually reassessing its own beliefs, traditions and structures, so too the study of history must unquestionably include religious phenomena within its purview. In the first article of the nascent *Journal of Religion* in 1921, he makes an eloquent plea for this mutual acceptance.[85] This basic view is later amplified and documented in *The Christian Philosophy of History*.[86] Case stands in opposition to the assumption that the religious factor should be excluded when doing history. This is just as imbalanced as analyzing all of history under the single category of politics. Any historian concerned with the life of common humanity in its entire spectrum cannot exclude religion:

> Within this widening of vision the historian is no longer content to center attention simply upon political happenings. The scope of his observation

<hr>

[83] Ibid., 238–39.
[84] Ibid., 238.
[85] Case, "Historical Study of Religion," 3.
[86] Case, *History*, 56–76.

enlarges to include those common daily interests which have characterized the life of men in general at all times. But no one of these interests has been more conspicuous or persistent than religion. Of humanity's past it can still be said with a large measure of truth that "a man's religion is the chief fact with regard to him—a man's or a nation of men's[.]" Therefore the study of religion falls properly and of necessity within the domain of the historian.[87]

It is this spiritual element, as feeding into the complex elements in history, which Case identifies as that from which the ultimate meaning and significance of history is derived.[88]

Conclusion: The Socio-Historical Method in Factorial Profile

Although many of the figures associated with the Chicago School—including Shirley Jackson Case—are often quite reflective about methodological issues, none ever sought to define precisely or delineate specifically the nature of the common method of the School, the socio-historical method. Within this and the previous chapter, various factors which characterize the socio-historical method as it occurred in both phases of Case's career have been noted. In the end, it is these factors which offer the best way of systematically defining or characterizing the socio-historical method itself. For the purpose of such a definition or characterization, some nine factors can be isolated and identified.

1. Historical

The socio-historical method is founded on the premise that not only are humanity, society, culture and religion in and of themselves historical phenomena, but also that history furnishes that milieu within which such realities can develop and come to the fore. No historical movement, society or religion ever emerged full-grown at the start. It is only under the impact of particular historical circumstances that this growth occurs. This is why "history may be said to make religion."[89] Furthermore, for Case it is ultimately human beings who make history.[90] When any of the above phenomena are placed within their respective historical perspectives, they are unable to claim normativeness for any later developments.

For Case, the historical method which is used to study both the New Testament and the history of Christianity must be the same basic type of historical method used to study secular texts and history. This methodological unity parallels his refusal to divide the historical realm into that which is natural and that which is supernatural. Historical methods which reflect this

---

[87] Case, "Historical Study of Religion," 2.
[88] See above, 70–71.
[89] Case, *History*, 164.
[90] See below, 92.

dichotomy, such as a providential or dualistic approach, are accordingly rejected.

2. Scientific-Empirical

Both the secular historian and the religious historian must have a scientific "method of procedure which is strictly inductive; all of his conclusions are to be derived from concrete and empirically verifiable data." The historian is not able to go beyond the "experimentally ascertainable facts."[91] He "shuns metaphysical speculation and worships at the shrine of empiricism."[92] This is possible because the moment social movements, be they cultural or religious, are acknowledged as historical they are regarded as facts open to empirical investigation. For these reasons, historians of religion must restrict themselves to the data discovered "in the actual personal experiences of the devotees of a religion."[93] One should proceed

> . . . under the conviction that religion can be best understood by giving first attention, not to its theoretical aspects, but to its actual historical manifestations, and when speculative interpretations and historical research meet on common grounds he will insist that all hypotheses be judged at the bar of his science.[94]

Because of its scientific empirical emphasis, the socio-historical method avoids the meta-historical views of both the providential and the dualistic views of history. This method operates only within the empirical domain of the human view of history.

3. Didactic

In line with its empirical stress, the socio-historical method rejects a priori judgments of how the past may be normative for the present. Thus, no standard or by-product of Christianity from the past can be normative for humanity in the present. However, if such a past product happens to meet the needs of persons in the present, then it may be utilized in the present. The past is didactic to the present, that is, it can offer models of past experience and explain how certain realities came into existence. Is nothing of the past normative for the present? Is Jesus to be considered merely as didactic? Case seems to make a parallel distinction; first, between the religion of Jesus and the religions about Jesus, and second, between the vitality inherent within secular and religious history and the by-products of this vitality. Therefore, it seems that while any by-product of Christianity, such as a particular Christology, could not be considered as a normative standard

---

[91] Case, "Historical Study of Religion," 8–9.
[92] Case, *History*, 57.
[93] Case, "Historical Study of Religion," 5, 11.
[94] Ibid., 9.

for later generations, the religion of Jesus or the vitality within religious history can be a stimulus for the generation of belief and action in others.

4. Social

The other element directly referred to in the title of the socio-historical method, and alluded to within the discussion of the social test, is the social factor. This factor can refer to at least two somewhat different things within the Chicago School: (a) the social or environmental setting of historical movements, and (b) the social or societal nature of any movement.

a. Social—The Environmental Setting

In seeking to evaluate particular past historical products in relation to their meeting the needs of that age or as providing expression for the religious experiences of Christians, the socio-historical method puts strong stress upon the knowledge of the past environments in which these products were formed.[95]

> From the point of view of historical study, life in relation to surroundings is the primal stuff out of which religions [and other social movements] evolve. They result from man's effort to secure and perpetuate the welfare of the group or of the individual in contact with environment, particularly in its less thoroughly mastered aspects.[96]

The historian "vigorously interrogates the environment in order to extract its secrets regarding the genetic forces" that have helped to make such social realities as nations and religions.[97] It is the concrete historical setting which furnishes "the greatest of stimuli for constructive and creative activity in the evolution" of humanity's spiritual and material development. However, this recognition of the importance of environmental stimulation for the creation of cultures and religions does not deny that there is operative a creative vitality within both cultures and religions.[98]

b. Social—The Societal Nature of Religion

Both Case and Mathews prefer to view the Christian religion as a social reality rather than as an abstract essence. Mathews states that "generic religion never existed apart from religions, and religions never existed except as interests and institutions of real people."[99] Accordingly, Christianity is coterminous with

---

[95] S. J. Case, "The Study of Early Christianity," in *A Guide to the Study of the Christian Religion*, ed. G. B. Smith (Chicago: University of Chicago Press, 1916) 243.

[96] Case, "Historical Study of Religion," 11.

[97] Ibid.

[98] Case, "Liberalism," 115.

[99] Shailer Mathews, "The Historical Study of Religion," in *A Guide to the Study of the Christian Religion*, 32.

> the actual life-process of the Christian society in its totality from its earliest beginnings down to the present moment. The history of Christianity is the story of religious living on the part of real people who from the first to last have constituted the membership of the Christian movement.[100]

Given this asssumption about the nature of religion, the socio-historical method seeks to go beyond historical products, such as biblical texts, creeds, doctrines and institutions, to the beliefs of the real people who themselves produced these products in response to the stimuli of their environment.

To reach adequately this social reality, historians have need not only of "trustworthy historical imagination," but also aid from the social sciences. They need the sociologist to provide information on the characteristic human motivations and activities. They need the aid of the psychologist to show how the mental interests of human beings may determine their behavior, and the anthropologist to clear up the contrast "between the presuppositions of a primitive age and those postulates by which . . . a man of the twentieth century is accustomed to regulate his conduct and thinking."[101]

5. Developmental or Evolutionary

All social realities which are historical in origin and responsive to their environment must be viewed as developmental or evolutionary rather than as static phenomena. Such historical phenomena "emerge and increase by a gradual process of growth from simpler to more elaborate forms. It is the business of the historian to follow the course of this evolutionary process from first to last."[102] "Thus history, which is in constant motion, may be marked by progressive development."[103] When Christianity is seen as a social movement rather than a collection of doctrines or creeds, then it can be said that:

> Christianity always had been and always would be a product of human evolution. Theology, like institutional developments and ritual formalities, was a product—perhaps sometimes only a by-product of the Christian religion.[104]

It is largely out of this methodological concern for historical realities as development that Case's own "theory" of the development of doctrine arises.

6. Vitalistic

The social process underlying all historical process is a vitalistic one. As previously noted, this vitalism arises from people's spiritual freedom and

---

[100] Case, "Religious Meaning of the Past," 586.
[101] Case, "Historical Study of Religion," 7, 13.
[102] Ibid., 10.
[103] Case, *History*, 148.
[104] Case, "Liberalism," 114.

ultimately gives history its final significance. In the human interpretation of history, this factor is the basis for hope, progress and the continual building up of human culture and civilization. "Thus one is led to realize that the character of future societies will also be determined, not by forces acting from without, but by a process of vital growth from within."[105] Every social movement and historical culture is seen to be an outgrowth of this fundamental human vitalism.

Christianity is also to be understood historically as the "story of religious living on the part of real people," that is, the "actual life-process of the Christian society."[106] "Christianity is primarily an affair of life, with varying characteristics according to the individuals and the circumstances which have determined its historical manifestations."[107] It is out of this vitalism of religious living that all historical products of Christianity can be understood to emerge. Ultimately, it is this same persistent vitality which is seen to be the "real secret of Christianity's life."[108] It is this vitalism which perpetuates Christianity and makes humanity historically righteous.[109]

7. Functional

Perhaps the most distinctive factor in Case's socio-historical method is its radical functionalism with respect both to its analysis of the past as past and its didactic use of the past in the present. All historical realities are to be evaluated solely in terms of their "functional efficiency" for the particular society which produced them. Thus, past historical products are authenticated by the degree to which they in fact met the needs within their particular situation. Similarly, the religious worth of particular beliefs, ideas or practices is estimated by their "functional significance in the life of the people by whom they had been espoused."[110]

> Every item in Christian belief at any period in history is a product of the experience and conviction of Christian people, and can be regarded as valid only so long as it serves adequately to express the sincerest convictions and deepest experiences of each new generation of Christian persons. This is the inescapable conviction to which we have been driven by the historical study of Christianity.[111]

Any historical vestige from the past found in the present can be evaluated by its functional significance for the present. When environments change,

---

[105] Case, "Historical Study of Religion," 15.
[106] Case, "Religious Meaning of the Past," 586.
[107] Case, *Evolution*, 1.
[108] Ibid., 41.
[109] Case, "Rehabilitation of Church History," 242.
[110] Case, "Liberalism," 112–13.
[111] Ibid., 115.

new pragmatic necessities are created and any idea or practice which is employed should be evaluated by the degree to which it can efficiently adjust to meet the pressure of these new necessities.[112]

8. Genetic

In line with its empirical emphasis, the socio-historical method of Case involves a continual search for the genetic forces in history. "To have real historical knowledge one must be familiar, not only with specific events, but also with the causal nexus underlying phenomena."[113] This concern to isolate the genetic forces of the causal nexus behind events is an attempt to understand the problem of "influence" and "continuity," that is, the linkage between historical events. This is in keeping with Case's whole evolutionary perspective and concern for history as an ongoing life process resulting from the social interplay within humanity of the spiritual and material elements. This same perspective prefers not to break history into periods or ages so that it is dealt with in a staccato fashion, "as if it were composed of watertight and separate compartments."[114] To do this would be to ignore the basic unity of history as assured by the "perpetuity of the human organism" and the permanence of the social and cultural environment.[115] At the same time, any historical method which attempts to deal only with isolated events, leaving the question of causes or continuity to "the realm of supernaturalism and metaphysical speculation," must also be avoided.[116]

9. Human Activism

In the final analysis, Case's socio-historical method views secular and religious history as the product of the utilization or non-utilization of human activism. "The human view of history seeks to portray the story of the past as a vital process of man's endeavor in every area of his activity."[117] All historical cultures, societies and religions witness to humanity's success or failure in utilizing its creative energy in these areas. The perpetuation of society, culture and Christianity is humanity's responsibility. The full responsibility for the future lies squarely upon humanity's shoulders.[118] The price of "making history" in these areas is "strenuous human living," "strenuous activism" and venturesome aggressiveness. In the secular understanding of history, this activism is seen to result in progress. In the religious understanding of history,

---

[112] Case, "Historical Study of Religion," 15–16; cf. *History*, 3.
[113] Case, "Historical Study of Religion," 5.
[114] Case, "Religious Meaning of the Past," 577.
[115] Case, *History*, 134.
[116] Case, "Historical Study of Religion," 15–16.
[117] Case, *History*, 90.
[118] Ibid., 91, 175.

this is seen as a "growing in historical righteousness."[119] "Activism, constantly renewed and persistently pursued so long as life remains, is the royal road to victory. . . . Religion today needs, not less divine guidance, but more human virility."[120]

Although extended analysis and evaluation of the socio-historical method of Case await the reader in the remaining chapters, a few brief critical comments are still in order at the conclusion of this factorial profile. With respect to Case's decided preference for the empirical over and against the metaphysical, it should be noted that at least since Augustine's work, *Against the Skeptics*, this argument might be recognized as circular in nature. Thus, to reject metaphysics, or philosophical views of the constitution of reality in general, would seem to mean that one would not be able to make any judgments with respect to empiricism. However, to make a judgment with respect to empiricism would be to enter the realm of metaphysical judgments. On this issue Bernard Meland has remarked that Case and his Chicago colleagues "bootlegged philosophy as much as they pooh-poohed it."[121] The problems attending the socio-historical method's claim to exclude metaphysics in particular and philosophy in general will receive extended critical attention in Chapter VI.

In dealing with the environmental influences upon Christianity, it is most certainly true that Case clearly posits a creative vitality within the heart of Christianity itself. Nonetheless, thematically the preponderance of Case's time is devoted to detailing the socio-cultural influences of various situations and periods *upon* Christianity rather than the opposite phenomenon, that is, Christianity's influence upon its various settings. Here Case is less adept than he might have been both in stating initially the nature of this dialectic and in studying concertedly both sides of it in history. At the same time this concentration on the one side of this dialectical process, that is, the influence of society and culture upon Christianity, may very well be due to the Chicago School's main extracurricular activity—battling against the fundamentalists' denial of all such influences in either the past or the present. The preference for the one side of this dialectic can be seen in the work of various practitioners of the socio-historical method as well. One has only to look to the predominant character of the essays in the Case Festschrift, *Environmental Factors in Christian History*, such as, Clyo Jackson's "The Hellenization of Jewish Messianism in Early Christianity," J. T. McNeill's "The Feudalism of the Church," and Richard McKeon's "Aristotelianism in Western Christianity."[122]

---

[119] Ibid., 145–46, 98.
[120] Ibid., 187.
[121] Bernard Meland, Discussion Vanderbilt Conference.
[122] Cf. McNeill, *Environmental Factors in Christian History*, 35–52.

With respect to the functionalism motif, while it can be found throughout Case's works, its sweep seems discernably broader and stronger toward the end of his scholarly career. Thus, in *The Christian Philosophy of History* (1943) this motif seems to have supplanted Case's earlier emphasis upon the centrality of the personal religion of Jesus for later believers.[123] Unfortunately, accompanying this shift there is no explicit or systematic discussion by Case of whether the personal religion of Jesus might serve as an ongoing basis for meeting functionally the needs of the continuing Christian communities. If anything, such a reference seems now to be rejected implicitly as a normative use of the past. By the same token, however, the possibility of a didactic role for Jesus is retained.[124]

[123] This emphasis is still central in *Jesus: A New Biography* (1927).
[124] Cf. Case, *History*, 3.

V

SOURCES OF THE SOCIO-HISTORICAL METHOD

There was a great sturdiness about his [Case's] intellect, and it will surprise me if . . . at any stage he relied on any author or coterie for his method and leading ideas. . . . He left the impression that as an historian he was nobody's disciple.

–John T. McNeill

Having isolated and identified the various major factors within the socio-historical method of Shirley Jackson Case, some estimation of the origins of the method with respect to particular possible influences should be made. Such an initial examination might prove especially valuable in weighing the accuracy of some scholarly assessments of this method. Furthermore, a method which attempted to understand religious beliefs by placing them against the horizon of sources and influences deserves similarly to be so placed and assessed.

The structure of this chapter's considerations falls into two parts: (1) possible German influences, and (2) possible American influences. In discussing all such influences, certain fundamental distinctions should be kept in mind. Direct comment or acknowledgment of influences by a principal party will be distinguished from thematic parallels and in turn from judgments by secondary parties. While each of these types of evidence has its own merits, it is important not to confuse one with the other. Several examples of where such a confusion has occurred in the past will be examined.

Possible German Influences

Introduction: Germanization of American Education

From the beginning of the seventeenth century onwards, the ideal of foreign education and travel was one strongly urged upon Americans, especially those engaged in maintenance of European aristocratic ideals.[1] Specific evidence of the determinative influence of German theological and historical scholarship, particularly in the nineteenth century, has recently been documented thoroughly in a study entitled *The German Historical School*

---

[1] Daniel J. Boorstin, *America and the Image of Europe* (New York: Meridian Books, 1960) 48.

in American Scholarship.[2] This work argues that the most intensive Germanization of American higher education occurred in the latter part of the last century and is reflected in the shift in America beyond colleges towards newly founded graduate schools.[3] These new graduate institutions were based in large part on the German university model. An important consequence for the teaching profession in America was a shift away from the ideal of the professor as teacher toward the ideal of the professor as professional research specialist. Such shifts in turn have significant ramifications for the entire educational support system. As the teacher becomes the researcher, the supporting institution becomes more research oriented, with a corresponding concern for the publication of such research. Accordingly, there arises the need for appropriate vehicles of communication. "The continued regular publication of the results of research led to the founding of scholarly and scientific periodicals, once more of the German example, by professional associations, university presses, or university departments."[4] By the turn of the twentieth century, faculty members at the University of Chicago could look not only to the University of Chicago Press as a means of publication but also to the *American Journal of Sociology, The American Journal of Theology, The Biblical World* and other journals.

The significant value which Americans placed upon German education in the nineteenth century is dramatically evident in the scholarly migrations of the American graduate student. Between 1820 and 1920, from nine to ten thousand Americans studied at German universities. Until the 1880s, the major areas of specialization chosen by these students were, in order of preference, medicine, law and theology. Shortly after the 1880s, theology displaced law in second place. One scholar has estimated that between 1875 and 1915, over 50 percent of America's leading liberal theologians had studied in German universities.[5]

It was true that nearly all the faculty of the Divinity School of the University of Chicago in the early 1900s had studied in Germany.[6] Harper himself had studied in Germany before assuming the presidency of the University. He in turn made this a precondition for hiring Edgar J. Goodspeed. Later Goodspeed himself made this a similar precondition for the addition of

---

[2] Jurgen Herbst, *The German Historical School in American Scholarship* (New York: Cornell University Press, 1965). Cf. Richard J. Storr, "German Influences," in *The Beginnings of Graduate Education in America* (Chicago: University of Chicago Press, 1953) Chapter III, 15–28.

[3] In 1918, William Adams Brown referred to this process as "the Prussianization of knowledge." Cf. Brown's review of *The Guide to the Study of the Christian Religion* in *The American Journal of Theology* 22 (1918) 443.

[4] Herbst, *German Historical School*, 38.

[5] William R. Hutchinson, *American Protestant Thought: The Liberal Era* (New York: Harper & Row, 1968) 7.

[6] At its beginnings the entire University of Chicago faculty included 14 German Ph.D.'s and 21 American Ph.D.'s (Storr, *Beginnings*, 76).

Ernest Cadman Colwell to the New Testament Department. Albion Small had arranged for Shailer Mathews to study political history and economics at Berlin. G. B. Foster had studied at Göttingen and Berlin. G. B. Smith had pursued studies under Wilhelm Hermann and Hermann Lotze at Marburg. S. J. Case did postdoctoral work under Adolf Jülicher at Marburg and Adolf von Harnack at Berlin in 1910. German universities were favorite locations for American professors on sabbatical. In 1914, Case was ready to join his wife in Germany for an academic sabbatical when he was prevented from doing this by the outbreak of World War I.

The advent of this war contributed directly to a marked diminution of student migrations to Germany. At the same time there were some parallel factors which also contributed significantly to this decline. For example, there was the pronounced growth of American graduate schools, now offering graduate studies in areas previously available only on the other side of the Atlantic. As the war progressed, it had a marked effect on the fall from grace in America of many previously adhered to German cultural ideals. At the same time there was a corresponding development of American intellectual independence. These last two trends are both evident in an article appearing in 1918 in *The Biblical World* entitled "The Paradox of Modern Biblical Criticism." The author, Louis Wallis, sets out a very critical reappraisal of German *Lehrfreiheit*, concluding that as a cultural ideal German academic freedom can be quite deceptive. It is pointed out that this supposed freedom ceased when the German academician stepped into the pulpit. "The so-called 'academic freedom' enjoyed by these professors is freedom to disseminate their ideas to scholars."[7] In reality modern Biblical scholarship is not allowed to be popularized, let alone preached from a pulpit. When a professor preaches he becomes the representative of orthodoxy and is subject to autocratic heresy laws. Readers of a sister publication, *The American Journal of Theology*, were familiar with this discussion since the effects of the Prussian heresy law of 1906 upon academic areas had been discussed by Errett Gates in two articles in recent numbers of this journal.[8]

Even though there was a devaluation of German cultural ideals, it should not be thought that either German educational or theological models yielded their preeminent status altogether. While student migrations in the early part of this century fell off in the fields of law and medicine, they continued for some time within the field of theology. It was still the assumed conventional wisdom that the Germans set the standards which others sought to rival or surpass. Only well past the midpoint of the twentieth century would the ideal

---

[7] Louis Wallis, "The Paradox of Modern Biblical Criticism," *The Biblical World* 52 (1918) 41ff.

[8] Errett Gates, "The New Prussian Heresy Law and Its Workings," *The American Journal of Theology* 16 (1912) 241–55; and Errett Gates, "Another Case of Discipline in the Prussian Church," *The American Journal of Theology* 17 (1913) 89–93.

of theological study in Germany lose its special normative status in American Protestant and Catholic academic circles.[9]

There is some evidence to indicate that the New Testament Department of the Divinity School of the University of Chicago sought consciously to assert their own scholarly autonomy during the second decade of this century. However, the initial form of this autonomy was little less than a veiled attempt to equal or outdistance the Germans. In this respect, Burton's claim that the New Testament Department at Chicago was the largest in the world has already been noted. In 1915, the department as a whole launched an appeal to university authorities for additional funds to subsidize the publication of the new works of the members of that department, citing the postwar period as promising an optimum opportunity for the expansion of American scholarship, especially since funds would not be so easily available to their German counterparts after the war.[10]

Another example of this attempt to equal German university standards is evidenced in the keen sense of satisfaction with which favorable comments or comparisons between Chicago and German universities were received. For instance, Goodspeed made a special point to write Burton, who was in China at the time, to tell him that his temporary replacement, Professor Karl Clemens, had spoken "most appreciately of the quality of man in his classes as compared with those at Bonn."[11] Clemens himself, in writing Burton, broadened the compliment:

> I began my lectures on the 1st of October and enjoy this work very much. The students seem to understand me fairly well and take a great interest in the subjects I am discussing. I think your way of conducting classes is much better than ours; we ought to learn from you in this as in many other respects.[12]

---

[9] Such study would seem to have retained its status somewhat longer for American Catholics than for Protestants. Perhaps, having arrived somewhat later at a confident assessment of their own indigenous theological resources, this group continued to think of German universities, along with their Belgian, Italian and French analogues, as "the" place to receive a "real" theological education until some time after the events of Vatican II. Of course this is not to deny the vestigial normativity still often associated by both American Catholics and Protestants with contemporary German theological figures.

[10] Letter, E. D. Burton to President Judson, March 2, 1915, University of Chicago Archives, Burton Letter File. Such referrals to German standards were not limited to the University of Chicago's Divinity School. Professor John U. Nef some years ealier remarked with respect to his own field: "I am really convinced that it will be possible to develop a school of Chemistry at Chicago comparable to the best in Germany." See Richard J. Storr, *Harper's University: The Beginnings* (Chicago: University of Chicago Press, 1966) 72.

[11] Letter, Edgar J. Goodspeed to E. D. Burton, November 30, 1908, University of Chicago Archives, Burton Letter File.

[12] Letter, Karl Clemens to E. D. Burton, October 9, 1908, University of Chicago Archives, Burton Letter File. Clemens was held in great esteem by the Chicago School. After the works of Harnack which received the greatest number of reviews in *The American Journal of Theology* (29), the works of Clemens were those most often reviewed (14).

The eastward cast of the eyes of some Chicago School figures was more pronounced than others. Goodspeed in particular seems to have been extremely conscious of any favorable mention that the School or its members might receive in Germany. It was with obvious pride that he recounted such an instance to Burton:

> I saw a brief and favorable notice of Miss Thompson's thesis in Theol. Lit. blatt (or -Zeitung) by H. Holtzmann (not H. J., I think) of Baden. It was prefaced by a flattering reference to our four selves, or rather our "wohl bekannte Namen"![13]

In a similar situation, it was typical of Case to refer to such German acknowledgment of his work as "slight yet favorable recognition . . . perhaps not worth mentioning."[14] It would be interesting to examine European periodicals and correspondence to determine to what extent the European theological community, particularly in Germany, was aware of the work of the Chicago School.[15]

In general, at Chicago there was a deep concern to maintain a comprehensive awareness of the latest developments in German theology. This is evidenced both in the works chosen for review as well as in the selection of guest lecturers. Robert Funk has remarked that it seems that the early Chicago School was out to review virtually every significant theological work fresh off the German presses.[16] Looking at a list of Case's own copious book reviews, it can be seen that nearly 60 percent of his reviews from 1908 to 1911 dealt with German works.[17] This intense interest in German scholarship is also evident in the regular series of guest lecturers funded by the Divinity

---

[13] Letter, Edgar J. Goodspeed to E. D. Burton, August 22, 1908, University of Chicago Archives, Burton Letter File.

[14] Letter, S. J. Case to E. D. Burton, December 7, 1911, University of Chicago Archives, Burton Letter File.

[15] A number of assorted comments by European scholars can be found in the archives of the Chicago School itself, including judgments by Karl Clemens, B. H. Streeter, Caspar Rene Gregory, and others. Ernst Troeltsch in a footnote in his article "The Dogmatics of the Religionsgeschichtliche Schule" compared his work with that of Foster's *The Finality of the Christian Religion.* See Ernst Troeltsch, "The Dogmatics of the Religionsgeschichtliche Schule," *The American Journal of Theology* 17 (1913) 11. Ludwig Köhler in an article on Formgeschichte made a similar favorable reference to Case's work on *The Historicity of Jesus.* See Ludwig Köhler, "The Meaning and Possibilities of *Formgeschichte*," *The Journal of Religion* 8 (1928) 612. These two references, of course, could have been made out of editorial courtesy rather than out of real interest. In some instances mere biographical references can be quite tangential if not plainly inaccurate. For example, Goodspeed noted that one of Case's early articles in *The Journal of American Theology* was "cited in a recent Catholic book from Paris, at the head of the 'inoffensive' list of auteurs Catholiques—'Case, S. J.'—What a thing it is to have significant initials!" Letter, Edgar J. Goodspeed to E. D. Burton, June 1910, University of Chicago Archives, Burton Letter File.

[16] Funk, Discussion Vanderbilt Conference.

[17] Jennings, *Bibliography*, 9–11.

School during Mathews' tenure as Dean. A significant number of these lecturers were from German universities, including such men as Karl Clemens, Gustav Krüger, Karl Meyer, Adolph Deissmann, Arthur Tissius and others. However, when such guests began to lecture, regardless of any mythical status which they may have had previously, members of the Chicago School were not hesitant to demythologize the abilities of such guests, as will be noted shortly.

Anyone wishing to argue independence of thought as the goal of the Chicago School in this period will first have to concede that for most Chicago figures a thorough knowledge of German scholarship was a *sine qua non* for embarking on their own work, and in some cases it was a continuing standard against which their work was to be measured.

The above discussion will serve, it is hoped, to set out the general context of the relationship of American higher education to German ideals and scholarship. However, to narrow further the focus upon the Chicago School and the possible German influences upon the origins of the socio-historical method of Case, there must be a more detailed discussion of specific possible German influences.

German Scholarship and the Socio-Historical Method of S. J. Case

In entering a discussion of possible specific ties between individual German movements and the origins of the socio-historical method, it might be well to summarize and illustrate briefly the major opinions on this subject. In general, these opinions fall roughly into two groups, the one viewing the relationship as a straightforward intellectual paternity, the other stressing varying degrees of independence.

A vituperative illustration of the first judgment can be found in the conclusion reached by the opponents of the Chicago School in the middle of the Modernist-Fundamentalist controversy in the 1920s. Thus, the *Minneapolis Daily Mirror* on May 24, 1920, under the banner headline "Modernist Would Pull God Off Throne, Riley Avers," quoted W. B. Riley, the noted fundamentalist, about the paternity of American modernism being traceable to German rationalism. "The Sampson of modernism, blinded by theological fumes from Germany, feels for the pillars of the Christian temple and would fain tear the last one away and leave Christianity itself in utter collapse."[18] Six years later, Riley repeated this charge in *Inspiration or Evolution*: "To say that the New Theologian has brought his method from Germany, as well as his message, is to state the matter both truthfully and tersely."[19]

---

[18] *Minneapolis Daily Mirror*, May 24, 1920, 1–2.

[19] W. B. Riley, *Inspiration or Evolution* (Cleveland: Union Gospel Press, 1926) 138. This work is a marvelous example of well wrought invective. Note the way that Riley's attack on "that German philosophy" of Kant and Nietzsche, seen as accepting neither God nor the Scriptures, is interwoven with wartime metaphors: "It was that philosophy, adopted by Nietzsche

A more contemporary and scholarly illustration of this first judgment is Robert Funk's evaluation of the first generation of Chicago scholars centering around Harper and Burton:

> Beyond achieving high level competencies in the traditional biblical disciplines, the new high scholarship at Chicago also had to catch up with the Germans. This meant, above all, the mastery of "higher criticism." It was in this domain that Chicago scholarship represented little more than a rehearsal of German theories. . . . The first generation was so preoccupied with assembling credentials, catching up, and competing for the lay mind, that it had little time for attention to broader theological problems, including the problem of biblical authority.[20]

In his opinion of the later Chicago school, however, Funk joins the second group of interpretation which stresses various degrees of independence between Case's socio-historical method and possible German influences. The precise degree of independence stressed remains a matter of some debate within this second group. It is well to note that some of the members of this second group are themselves linked historically or intellectually with the Chicago School.

John T. McNeill falls within the latter group when he notes that Case "left the impression that as an historian he was nobody's disciple." Further, there seems to be little evidence "that at any stage he relied on any author or coterie for his method and leading ideas."[21] Robert Funk judges Case more radical than either Harper or Burton. Case "was his own man, a rigorous, unrelenting scholar and thinker, in pursuit of a distinctive methodology and a grand overview of history."[22] Bernard Meland maintains that the scholars in the Chicago School, once they were thoroughly familiarized with the German scene firsthand, returned to America and proceeded either to abandon what they had learned or adapt it to the "study of contemporary ends within a medium native to the American experience."[23]

---

and for a full thirty years made the basis of all German education that finally fruited in the late war, baptized the world in blood, gave birth to Bolshevism, wrought irreparable injustice to the doctrine of brotherhood, and left the whole earth wondering whether, after all, it had a God! Metaphysics was once described by a shrewd critic as 'a Scotch mist,' and another described 'psychology' as 'a modern mirage.' But it has remained for philosophy to prove itself 'a gas' more poisonous than any that Germany ever loosed against the Allies. It is claimed for certain fumes, thought and wrought out in Teutonic laboratories, that when released they took their way over tops and thru trenches and left, in their wake, thousands of young men suffocating, strangling, blackening, biting the dust and dying. . . . What these fumes were to physical men, modern philosophy is proving itself to be to men's souls." Riley, *Inspiration*, 257.

[20] Funk, "Watershed," 24.

[21] Letter, John T. McNeill to William J. Hynes, August 17, 1970.

[22] Funk, "Watershed," 15.

[23] Meland, "Reflections," 8.

James Luther Adams has observed that there are no "signs that Case was positively stimulated by anything going on in Germany."[24] For his part, Wilhelm Pauck has commented in a similar fashion that there is no evidence "that Case or his colleagues were consciously or intentionally dependent upon the Germans." At the same time, however, Pauck concedes that at least initially there was a strong Ritschlian cast to the work of a number of Chicago figures.[25]

To date, there is no evidence that Case himself ever commented explicitly on this general relationship question, although his essay on "Education in Liberalism" comes very near to doing so. At the same time, however, he did declare explictly his admiration of a posture of informed independence when he found it in others. Thus in 1923, while applauding B. W. Bacon and F. C. Porter, his former teachers at Yale, Case stated:

> Under such men, New Testament studies at Yale represented a position considerably in advance of that which prevailed at the English and Scottish universities and more in line with the work that was being carried on in Germany by, for example, Jülicher and the older Holtzmann. But this thorough acquaintance with world scholarship never degenerated into a mere echo of foreign opinions. When the biblical teachers at Yale spoke, it was to express conviction of their own, that had been reached in the full light of opinions held by their predecessors and contemporaries, but that represented in every instance a careful criticism and reworking of the materials and problems involved, or a piece of further investigation in some new section of the field.[26]

While explicit commentary by Case on the relationship of the origins of the socio-historical method to possible German influences is lacking, it could be argued by inference that his awarding of the above plaudits to others is reflective of the standards of scholarship which Case himself sought to maintain.

In order to examine the possibility of German influence analytically, several specific pertinent German movements will be viewed in some detail. These will include Neo-Kantianism, Ritschlianism and Adolf Harnack, the *Religionsgeschichtliche Schule* and Ernst Troeltsch, and *Formgeschichte*.

Neo-Kantianism

The influence of some of the members of the Southwestern School of Neo-Kantianism, especially Heinrich Rickert (1863–1936) and Wilhelm

---

[24] James Luther Adams, "The Relationship Between the Chicago School and the Continent," Address Vanderbilt Conference, 1969, privately possessed tape.

[25] Letter, Wilhelm Pauck to William J. Hynes, April 2, 1971.

[26] S. J. Case, "Contributions of the Yale Divinity School to Theological Literature," *The Centennial Celebration of the Founding of the Yale Divinity School* (New Haven: Yale University Press, 1922) 19–24.

Windelband (1848–1915), is very evident in the work of one member of the Chicago School, George Burman Foster. Foster's *The Finality of the Christian Religion* was quite closely linked both stylistically and intellectually with German scholarship in general and Neo-Kantianism in particular. For example, he not only adopts the Neo-Kantian distinction between nomothetic and ideographic, but also he is heavily indebted to Troeltsch for his own discussion of the essence of Christianity.[27] However, such obvious indebtedness should not be interpreted automatically as mere imitation. James Luther Adams has recently cautioned against such a simple presumption:

> Foster shows considerable independence and originality in his formulations of these methods and the critiques that they imply. The critique that he gives qualifies the distinction between the nomothetic and the ideographic in very subtle ways. I would say that anyone who has read in the last two decades the literature on the logic of the cultural sciences, the *Geisteswissenschaften*, and who also reads Foster, will find Foster making qualifications and criticisms which are very shrewd and subtle with respect to the definition of these two methods, especially with respect to the attempt to separate them. When you are studying human existence-personalities, only the one method is appropriate. He asks for a kind of mutuality of method.[28]

There is no evidence that any of the other members of the Chicago School were as directly influenced by Neo-Kantianism as was Foster. In turn, Foster's own influence upon other members of the Chicago group seems to have been equally limited. Interest in the philosophy of religion or a philosophical approach to the truth question was less characteristic of either Mathews or Case. In fact, as will be indicated shortly, Mathews seems to have counterposed such concerns as somewhat antithetical to being concerned with the growth of the Christian movement. In addition, the declared anti-metaphysical bias found in the socio-historical method as practiced by Case would seem clearly to distinguish this method from Foster's basic approach.

Nonetheless, there may have been some indirect influences of Neo-Kantianism upon Case, either through Foster or Ritschlianism. Thus, a possible thematic parallel between the terms nomothetic and ideographic, especially as applied to history by the Neo-Kantians and Troeltsch, and what Case calls "normative" and "didactic" within the socio-historical method will be discussed. However, nowhere does Case himself enter into any explicit discussion of this possible thematic congruence between the socio-historical method and Neo-Kantian thought.

---

[27] George Burman Foster, *The Finality of The Christian Religion* (2nd ed.; Chicago: University of Chicago Press, 1906). In particular see Chapter VII, "The Essence of the Christian Religion: The Problem of Method," 279–324.

[28] Adams, "Relationship."

Ritschlianism and Adolf Harnack

The pervasiveness of a Ritschlian influence upon many members of the Chicago School, including Case, is widely acknowledged. As Pauck has noted, many Chicago figures began their careers as Ritschlians. This should not be too surprising given the strength with which Ritschlianism was in vogue in Germany during the period when many of the Chicago scholars did their graduate work there. In general, such characteristic Ritschlian stresses as value judgments as the source of faith-knowledge, the centrality of the person of Jesus, the community as the fundamental religious unit, religious experience as more basic than doctrine, metaphysics not being equated with religion and so forth are familiar themes within the thought of such Chicago thinkers as Mathews, Case, Smith and others. Smith, as a noted disciple of Wilhelm Herrmann, came to be labeled an "American Ritschlian."[29]

The continuing deep interest of the Chicago School in Ritschl and Ritschlianism is very evident within the pages of *The American Journal of Theology* (1897–1920). There are eight articles alone specifically in this area, a very high number of articles for a single area for this journal. The articles deal with Ritschl's metaphysical and theological presuppositions, his use of value judgments, his criterion of religious truth, and the difference between theoretical and religious knowledge. Beyond these eight there were other related articles such as the one by Julius Kaftan in 1900, entitled "Authority as a Principle of Theology."[30]

While these Chicago figures often explicitly conceded the influence of Ritschlianism upon them, they just as often took pains to demonstrate just how far they had moved beyond Ritschlianism.[31] In particular, they attempted to go beyond Ritschlianism with a more thoroughgoing functionalism and by initiating a wider discussion with the natural and social sciences regarding the question of the proper method of studying religion. According to Pauck, the latter activity arose out of an embarrassment by Smith and others at Chicago "that Ritschl and his German pupils and followers did not give them any tools to come to terms with the world-views stimulated by the natural sciences."[32] A detailed study of each Chicago figure's relationship to Ritschlianism might prove a most interesting project, if understandably one

---

[29] "Ritschlianism," *American Encyclopedia of Religion*, ed. Vergilius Ferm (New York: Philosophical Library, 1945) 664–65.

[30] Julius Kaftan, "Authority as a Principle of Theology," *The American Journal of Theology* 4 (1900) 673–733.

[31] See Shailer Mathews, "Gerald Birney Smith," *The Divinity Student* 6/2 (1929) 33–41; Shailer Mathews, *New Faith for Old*, 42ff.; G. B. Smith, "George Burman Foster," *The Biblical World*, 53/2 (1919) 181–183; G. B. Smith, "Appeal to Christ," *Current Christian Thinking* (Chicago: University of Chicago Press, 1928) 97–125.

[32] Letter, Wilhelm Pauck to William J. Hynes, April 2, 1971.

beyond the present scope of this work.[33] For this reason, extended comment must be virtually restricted to S. J. Case's relationship to Ritschlianism.

In his essay "Education in Liberalism," Case deals with his own earlier indebtedness to Ritschlianism. In commenting upon his studies, probably at Yale Divinity School just after the turn of the century, he states:

> Ritschlianism was the prevailing type of theology taught in our classrooms. The moral and spiritual ideals of Jesus and Paul were thought to constitute the heart of the New Testament message. Thus it was easy to believe that "value judgments" attested by a present-day religious consciousness were reproducing strictly the actual content of the religion that had been held by the first and best representatives of Christianity.[34]

As Case became subsequently critical of the underlying assumption that such contemporary value judgments reproduce the original content of Christianity, he found himself moving significantly beyond both Ritschlianism and his own earlier position. In becoming doubtful whether such value judgments really reproduce the actual religion of Jesus and in reacting to what he saw as an unacceptable essence logic in Harnack, Case went notably beyond the position held during his tenure as a professor of New Testament and still visible as late as his 1927 *Jesus: A New Biography.*

Case's own contribution was to sever the Ritschlian linkage between contemporary value judgments and the religion of Jesus. He retained both elements but dissolved their linkage. The absence of such a linkage is perhaps most obvious in Case's last major work, *The Christian Philosophy of History* (1945). Here the religion of Jesus retains no normative character other than that of being potentially inspiring to later Christians. The value judgment schema has been subsumed under the functionalism of the socio-historical method. In this new form, the issue is now to what extent any given expression of Christianity could be considered to have been functional within its particular environment, or the extent to which such an expression was efficient in meeting the needs of the particular group. In short, Case's later position lacks the earlier Ritschlian surety that one's contemporary religion is the same as that of Jesus in the first century. On the contrary, for Case at this point, Jesus would seem to be but one embodiment of the Christian religion,

---

[33] For an excellent and detailed study of the impact of Ritschlian theology upon American theological thought, see Bernard Meland, "Appeal to Christ in Present Day Religious Interpreters," (Ph.D. dissertation, University of Chicago, 1929). This work also contains a bibliography of everything on Ritschlian theology appearing in English from 1872 until 1915. As to various contemporary understandings of what was meant by Ritschlian theology, see Albert Temple Swing, *The Theology of Albrecht Ritschl* (New York: Longmans, Green & Co., 1901) or John Kenneth Mozley, *Ritschlianism* (London: James Nisbet & Co., 1909) or the somewhat biased James Orr, *The Ritschlian Theology and the Evangelical Faith* (New York: Thomas Whittaker, 1897).

[34] Case, "Liberalism," 109.

an embodiment which is no more normative trans-temporally than any other.

It should be noted that on this and several other matters Case and Mathews parted Ritschlian company. Thus, Mathews retained a more characteristic Ritschlian linkage between the religion of Jesus and contemporary value judgments. It may be that Mathews' evangelical interests did not prepare him to accept as thoroughgoing a distinction between the normative and the didactic uses of the past as had Case. With respect to metaphysics, however, Mathews showed himself somewhat less Ritschlian than Case. Mathews was far more willing to find a metaphysical referent in both religion and theology with which Case would have been most uncomfortable:

> Religion is a word of experience, but it has a correlate in an extra-experiential reality which is a dominating factor in the situation out of which religion develops. . . . A theology in the nature of the case must therefore contain its meta-experiential elements.[35]

To a significant degree, Case's break with Ritschlianism may mark the transition from the partially developed socio-historical method of Case as the New Testament scholar to the fully developed socio-historical method of Case as the historian of Christianity.

With respect to Adolf Harnack, Case's book reviews and some of his major writings reflect a strong familiarity with many of Harnack's works. Indeed, Case's name appears in the front of Harnack's Festschrift in 1921, as one who had studied with Harnack.[36] Although he himself never explicitly acknowledged having studied with Harnack in Berlin, this must have occurred during his postgraduate work in Germany in 1910.

Wilhelm Pauck closely ties Case with a particular disciple of Harnack: "Case was a student of Gustav Krüger, one of Harnack's earliest pupils, a Ritschlian, and a persuaded theological liberal."[37] "I remember clearly that Case had a high respect for Krüger and I am sure that he told me that he had studied with Krüger in Germany."[38] Krüger was visiting professor at Chicago in either 1927 or 1928 and resided at the apartment of Case who was then on sabbatical.

While Harnack and Case obviously shared a mutual interest in the history of early Christianity, there seems to be little ground for supposing that the former influenced in any positive manner the latter's formation of the socio-historical method. On the contrary, some of Case's work was written in

---

[35] Mathews, "Historical Study of Religion," 46ff.

[36] As quoted by G. Wayne Glick, *The Reality of Christianity* (New York: Harper & Row, 1967) 36, n. 1.

[37] Letter, Wilhelm Pauck to William J. Hynes, April 2, 1971.

[38] Letter, Wilhelm Pauck to William J. Hynes, September 21, 1975. Other than this observation there is no formal evidence of Case's having ever studied with Krüger.

reaction against aspects of Harnack's thought. Accordingly, the functionalism of the socio-historical method may have partially been a response to the perceived essentialism of Harnack.[39]

Religionsgeschichtliche Schule and Ernst Troeltsch

Case was very sympathetic to and informed about various developments represented within the boundaries of the *Religionsgeschichtliche Schule*. The school and its members found repeated and detailed mention in Case's first two major works, his later autobiographical essay, and many of his book reviews.[40]

"The problem of the so-called *Religionsgeschichtliche Schule* . . . is to relate the Christianity of the New Testament times to its immediate religious environment in the popular life of the Graeco-Roman world."[41] Such a general description could easily be said to resemble Case's own socio-historical method. In fact, the *sine qua non* of both approaches is the admission that "the Christian movement had gathered unto itself, even in the early stages of its evolution, many accretions, first from its Jewish and later from its gentile environment."[42]

On occasion, this general similarity of approach led Case to comment upon the proper uses of the history-of-religions approach whether it be at the hands of those within or outside the *Religionsgeschichtliche Schule* as such. For example, with respect to the latter, Case took sharp exception to Arthur Drews' "misuse" of the history-of-religions approach in attempting to reason from the evidence of religious syncretism within Christianity to the conclusion that Christianity itself must therefore lack its own integrity and autonomous character:

> No amount of parallelism, not even demonstrable "borrowing," disposes of the genuineness of these [New Testament] writings unless it can be demonstrated that the personal note contained in them is not genuine and that the idea of newness is itself fictitious.[43]

For Case, the logic behind Drews' approach is quite similar to that behind attempts either to minimize acknowledged "foreign admixtures" or to claim that such additions are strictly limited to minor externals which do not disturb

---

[39] See Chapter II, 20ff.

[40] See Case, *Historicity of Jesus*, 42ff., 63ff.; Case, *Evolution of Early Christianity*, 108ff., 191ff.; Case, "Liberalism," 113ff.

[41] Case, *Evolution*, 191–92.

[42] Case, "Liberalism," 113.

[43] Case, *Historicity*, 68. For a recent revisitation to the issues of the debate occasioned by Drews, see Brian Gerrish, "Jesus, Myth, and History: Troeltsch's Stand in the 'Christ-Myth' Debate," *The Journal of Religion* 55 (1975) 13–35. For an example of the continuing problem of argumentation from parallels, see William J. Hynes' review of Morton Smith, *Jesus the Magician*, in *Christian Century*, July 19, 1979, 714–15.

an underlying essence. In all these examples, the common hidden assumption seems to be that to admit any significant outside influences upon Christianity would in fact endanger its integrity and substance.

For his part, Case holds the contrary assumption that the integrity of Christianity does not rest upon what may or may not have been borrowed from elsewhere, but rather upon the use to which such borrowings were put. At this point, we have once again come to Case's functionalism:

> Religious worth was not to be measured by the source from which ideas or practices had been originally derived, but to know their origin and history enabled the student to appraise their functional significance in the life of the people by whom they had been espoused.[44]

Within his book reviews, Case occasionally took detailed exception to the positions of some of those individuals formally identified with this school. For example, in 1914, under the general title "New *Religionsgeschichtliche* Studies on Christian Origins," he reviewed Eduard Norden's *Agnostos Theos: Untersuchungen zur Formengeschichte religiöser Rede*, Wilhelm Bousset's *Kyrios Christos: Geschichte des Christusglaubens von den Anfängen des Christentums bis Irenaeus* and Johannes Weiss' *Das Urchristentum*, Volume 1, in *The American Journal of Theology*. Case passes quickly over Weiss' work since it is only a partial installment of a larger work. Norden's work

> proceeds mainly upon a study of words and phrases gleaned from the "byways and hedges" of Greek and Latin literature, rather than from a comprehensive investigation of religious movements within the life of the times. This feature constitutes the strength of the volume as well as its weakness.[45]

The limitations are those characteristic of all word studies or literary-form studies: "A too purely lexical study may betray one into the danger of becoming so intent upon viewing the trees as to be unable to see the forest." There is an equal need to grant time to such factors as "soil, climate and environment" and to understand the whole background of syncretistic religious life in the Graeco-Roman world. These criticisms are basically those expanded and amplified in *Jesus: A New Biography* a decade later, when Case discusses *Literaturgeschichte* and *Formgeschichte*.[46]

In reviewing Bousset's work, Case again applauds the use of the general history-of-religions method whose "correctness of expounding Christianity in the light of conditions within the Graeco-Roman world can no longer be

---

[44] Case, "Liberalism," 113.

[45] S. J. Case, "New *Religionsgeschichtliche* Studies on Christian Origins," *The American Journal of Theology* 18 (1914) 440–45.

[46] Case, *Jesus: A New Biography*, 56. See above Chapter III, 40ff.

questioned."[47] At the same time, however, he takes issue with particular details of Bousset's conclusions. Thus, "Paul has been made too un-Jewish and too uneschatological" and "primitive Christians have been made too un-'spiritual' and too unecstatic."[48] This is due to Bousset's practice of reading the early period of Christianity through the lens of the later period in which James presided over the church at Jerusalem, and the earlier primitive enthusiasm had waned after the more aggressive spirits had moved on.

Within the boundaries of the *Religionsgeschichtliche Schule*, Ernst Troeltsch was widely regarded as its systematic theologian, as he himself acknowledged in an article in *The American Journal of Theology* in 1913.[49] S. J. Case and G. B. Smith, as joint editors of this journal, manifested a strong general interest in the matters treated by this school. Thus, in addition to Troeltsch's article, they also elicited and published in the same year two other articles from members of this school, Johannes Weiss' essay on "The Significance of Paul for Modern Christians," and Hugo Gressmann's essay on "The Sources of Israel's Messianic Hope."[50]

Case's own general interest is also reflected in his own book reviews between 1911 and 1915, during which period he reviewed at least seven works by major members of the *Religionsgeschichtliche Schule*, including three works by Johannes Weiss, two works by Bousset, and one by Troeltsch.[51]

While there was some general interest in Troeltsch's ideas within the Chicago group, as indicated by the presence of his own article as well as two

[47] Case, "New *Religionsgeschichtliche* Studies," 444.

[48] Ibid., 444–45.

[49] Ernst Troeltsch, "The Dogmatics of the 'Religionsgeschichtliche Schule,'" 1. Pauck recalls that Troeltsch discounted the importance of systematic theology even though that was the chair which he held, cf. Wilhelm Pauck, *Harnack & Troeltsch* (New York: Oxford University Press, 1968) 63. This was not Troeltsch's first article to appear in an American journal. That honor, by three months, went to the *Harvard Theological Review*. Ernst Troeltsch, "Empiricism and Platonism in the Philosophy of Religion," *Harvard Theological Review* 5 (1912) 401–2. In 1905, Troeltsch had journeyed to America to the World's Fair in St. Louis, accompanied by Max Weber, to deliver an address entitled "Psychology and Epistemology in the Science of Religion." Three years later, he published two lengthy entries, entitled respectively "Contingency" and "Historiography," in the *Encyclopedia of Religion and Ethics*, ed. James Hastings (New York: Charles Scribner & Sons, 1908) 1:87–89; 6:716–23.

[50] Johannes Weiss, "The Significance of Paul for Modern Christians," *The American Journal of Theology* 17 (1913) 352–62; Hugo Gressmann, "The Sources of Israel's Messianic Hope," *The American Journal of Theology* 17 (1913) 173–95.

[51] During this period, Case reviewed Weiss' *Die Aufgaben der neutestamentlichen Wissenschaft in der Gegenwart* in *The American Journal of Theology* 15 (1911) 286–89, *Das Johannesevangelium* in *The American Journal of Theology* 17 (1913) 288–91, *Das Urchristentum* in *The American Journal of Theology* 18 (1914) 440–45, and *Jüdisch-christlicher Schulbetrieb in Alexandria und Rom* in *The American Journal of Theology* 19 (1915) 599–600. Case also briefly reviewed Troeltsch's *Die Bedeutung der Geschichtlichkeit Jesu für den Glauben* in *The American Journal of Theology* 15 (1911) 626–28.

other articles about him in *The American Journal of Theology*, no major Chicago figure at this point other than Foster seems to have been significantly influenced by Troeltsch.[52] This may seem somewhat surprising given the Chicago School's awareness of German theologians, particularly those associated with the history-of-religions group, of which Troeltsch was an acknowledged member. It is particularly puzzling since Case and Troeltsch are both so closely identified with social approaches to the history of Christianity. Pauck notes his own astonishment that "neither Case nor his colleagues, particularly Mathews and G. B. Smith, did not study Troeltsch more closely and that they made no use of his Sozial-Lehren."[53]

> Why was Troeltsch not a more important figure among the Chicago School? Troeltsch was really their man. He was closer to their thinking than most of them [other German theologians]. And the socio-historical method, whatever was meant by it by Mathews, G. B. Smith, or Case and the others, would have been supported by Troeltsch. They hardly ever referred to him in their writings, and they hardly even spoke of him.[54]

In fact, Troeltsch's writings are cited fairly often within Case's works. Thus, both editions of *Die Absolutheit* (1902, 1912) were mentioned and discussed in Case's *Evolution* (1914).[55] In the same work, Troeltsch's *Die Soziallehren*

---

[52] Since Foster seems to have had little impact on the later members of the Chicago School, the possibility of Troeltsch's having influenced these through Foster would seem slight. A noteworthy extramural influence, however, can be seen in Foster's student, D. C. MacIntosh, who continued his mentor's active interest in Troeltsch. For example, see D. C. MacIntosh, "Troeltsch's Theory of Knowledge," *The American Journal of Theology* 23 (1919) 274–89. In turn, MacIntosh's students, Reinhold and H. Richard Niebuhr, were both enamored of Troeltsch and "have often acknowledged that their ways of handling theological problems were deeply determined by their study of Troeltsch's writings." Pauck, *Harnack & Troeltsch*, 43. H. Richard Niebuhr did his dissertation on Troeltsch's philosophy of religion in 1924 under MacIntosh. It is also interesting that Henry Nelson Wieman, a latecomer to the Chicago School in 1927 and identified with a subsequent methodological shift at Chicago, had himself studied for six months under both Troeltsch and W. Windelband at Heidelberg University. The restriction of Foster's influence within the Chicago School may also have been due in part to an antiphilosophical bias at work within many of the members of this group. This matter will be discussed in Chapter VI.

[53] Letter, Wilhelm Pauck to William J. Hynes, April 2, 1971. In a recent dissertation, Larry L. Greenfield shares this judgment about Smith's non-utilization of Troeltsch's *Social Teachings*. Cf. Larry L. Greenfield, "The Theology of Gerald Birney Smith" (Ph.D. dissertation, University of Chicago, 1978) 139. At the same time, however, Greenfield argues that Smith often cites Troeltsch's works and that there is some evidence of the latter's influence upon the former's Christology.

[54] Pauck, Discussion Vanderbilt Conference. Pauck goes on to suggest that one possible answer to this question might be the American preference for "plain talk" over and against the sometimes obscure style of Troeltsch's writings. As a person who studied under both Harnack and Troeltsch and later became a member of the Chicago School in the late 1920s, Pauck has rare qualifications from which to draw such comparisons.

[55] Case, *Evolution*, 14–15.

der christlichen Kirchen und Gruppen (1911) is also cited. This citation occurs again in Case's later *The Social Origins of Christianity* (1923).[56] Various portions of *Der Historismus und seine Probleme* (1922) are referred to in footnotes in *The Christian Philosophy of History* (1943).[57] However, the only work of Troeltsch reviewed formally by Case was the short essay, *Die Bedeutung der Geschichtlichkeit Jesu für den Glauben* reviewed in the same year as its appearance, 1911.[58] In his *Evolution*, Case also made reference to three articles by Troeltsch, "Dogmatik" and "Glaube und Geschichte" which had appeared in 1910 in *Die Religion in Geschichte und Gegenwart*, and a third article which had been published in *The American Journal of Theology*.[59]

Despite these bibliographical references to Troeltsch, Case devotes fewer than two pages to Troeltsch's ideas in his *Evolution*, and even fewer than that in *The Christian Philosophy of History*. His review of *Die Bedeutung der Geschichtlichkeit Jesu für den Glauben* is only nine lines *in toto*.

What grasp Case had of Troeltsch seems to have been based upon *Die Absolutheit*. On the basis of this, he judges Troeltsch a modified Hegelian for whom "the Absolute becomes less a predetermined quantum and more a product of historical growth."[60] Even though Troeltsch uses the history-of-religions method, considered so indispensable by Case for the study of Christianity, the latter finds an unacceptable agenda in the former's use of this method:

> It appears, however, that Christianity as a matter of fact is the best religion, and so has a just claim to the title "absolute." As yet its complete finality may not be fully established, but its development is surely moving toward this end. Enough of its distinctive characteristics have already emerged to furnish adequate grounds for faith in its ultimate absoluteness. So Troeltsch can speak of an "essential" Christianity in whose history the fundamental "ideal" is being realized through progress toward the "absolute goal."[61]

This judgment occurs in Case's *The Evolution of Early Christianity* in 1914, and can be found a year earlier in an article entitled "The Problem of Christianity's Essence" in *The American Journal of Theology*.[62] In keeping with

---

[56] Ibid., 70. Case, *Social Origins*, 255.

[57] Case, *History*, 60, 78.

[58] S. J. Case, "Recent Books on the Question of Jesus' Existence," *The American Journal of Theology* 15 (1911) 626–28.

[59] Case, *Evolution*, 14.

[60] Ibid., 13. James Luther Adams speaks of Troeltsch's position in *Absolutheit* as a form of "relativized Hegelianism" but with a meaning significantly different from what Case meant by "modified Hegelianism." Cf. James Luther Adams, "Introduction," in Ernst Troeltsch, *The Absoluteness of Christianity and the History of Religions*, trans. David Reid (Richmond: John Knox Press, 1971) 13.

[61] Case, *Evolution* 14.

[62] S. J. Case, "The Problem of Christianity's Essence," *The American Journal of Theology* 17 (1913) 553.

his writing regime, this article is incorporated verbatim into *The Evolution of Early Christianity*. Even though Case acknowledges Troeltsch's article which appeared slightly prior to his own in the same journal, there is no substantive use of Troeltsch's thought from the article. It is particularly curious that he did not note Troeltsch's ideas on the essence of Christianity which were not unlike his own:

> Thus the essence of Christianity can be understood only as the productive power of the historical Christian religion to create new interpretations—a power which lies deeper than any historical formulation which it may have produced. In this the essence of Christianity differs in different epochs, and is to be understood as something involved in the totality of its active influence.[63]

There is little evidence from which to respond in an explanatory manner to Pauck's perceptive observation that Case did not utilize either the content or the method of the *Soziallehren*. It may have been that Case's initial estimation of Troeltsch's thought on the basis of *Die Absolutheit* precluded further interest in other major works such as the *Soziallehren* and foreclosed the opportunity to discover the wealth of complementary themes in such works.[64]

If little can be said with respect to the causes of this lack of interface, something more might be said with respect to some of the opportunities which may have been lost by this omission. In general, given the preeminent status accorded both these figures in Europe and America respectively for their efforts toward understanding the history of Christianity from a social point of view, it must at the very least remain an irony of history that no direct, one-on-one exchange occurred between them.

Within a different setting it might be valuable to speculate in an extended way on what sort of scholarly exchange or clarifications might have occurred between the two had there been a fuller reciprocal awareness of each other's works. However, since the expressed purpose of the present limited format is to discuss pertinent possible sources of the socio-historical method, only the briefest of suggestions can be made here.

---

[63] Troeltsch, "The Dogmatics of the 'Religionsgeschichtliche Schule,'" 12–13.

[64] A noteworthy example of the dangers inherent in focusing upon any single work as representative of a creative evolving thinker can be seen in Case's and Mathews' view of Troeltsch. Thus, Case focused on portions of *Die Absolutheit* and thereafter avoided Troeltsch as an idealist too much taken with philosophy and metaphysics. Mathews on the other hand focused on Troeltsch's final work, *Christian Thought: Its History and Application* (1924) and, not unlike Friedrich von Hügel, worried whether Troeltsch's "stern realism" had led him too far away from the nomothetic! See Shailer Mathews, "Troeltsch's Last Work," *The Journal of Religion* 5 (1925) 325–27. Unfortunately, this limited knowledge of the sweep of Troeltsch's thought impeded both Case and Mathews from gaining a critical awareness of Troeltsch's significant explorations.

While both figures advocate understanding Christianity from a social and historical point of view, they differ significantly in their understanding of the nature of this process and would have at least initially taken strong exception to what they would have perceived as inherent defects in each other's point of view. When Case speaks of the social consequences attending Christianity, he is almost exclusively concerned about the direct effects of different social environments upon Christianity. On the other hand, Troeltsch understands by social consequences the direct effects which Christianity had upon surrounding social environments. He virtually rules out any such direct influences flowing in the opposite direction. "It is clear that the rise of Christianity is a religious and not a social phenomena [*sic*]. For although religion is interwoven with life as a whole, in development and dialectic it has an independent existence."[65]

These stances would seem to separate sharply Troeltsch and Case. One must not overlook each figure's motives, however. Case's stance is taken vis-à-vis the fundamentalists who seem to reject out-of-hand the notion of social influence upon Christianity. Accordingly, Case is intent upon demonstrating the myriad of ways in which successive social and cultural environments have shaped Christianity. Troeltsch, on the other hand, forms his arguments against those who seem to have fallen victim all too easily to the sociological premise of Emile Durkheim that religion is nothing else than transcendentalized social structures.[66] Accordingly, Troeltsch is intent upon retaining the inherently unique religious character of Christianity.

Unfortunately, lacking a detailed dialogue on this specific question between these two figures, it is exceedingly difficult to resolve whether these differences are in fact substantive, conceptual, or terminological. Some clarity may be gained from two other areas. Thus, it can be noted that both Troeltsch and Case share a similar tendency to speak of the essence of Christianity as an inner impulse. Case speaks of a "vitalism" and "strange recuperative power." Troeltsch speaks of an "inner productive power." For his part Case seems quite comfortable to have this understood in a quasi-Bergsonian fashion; Troeltsch, however, wishes to understand this as a distinctive a priori or as metaphysical in character.[67] Secondly, both men attempt to locate historical studies somewhere in a middle ground between that which is nomothetic and that which is ideographic.[68] This seems to be the role assigned to what Case

---

[65] Ernst Troeltsch, *The Social Teachings of the Christian Churches*, trans. Olive Wyon (New York: Macmillan Co., 1931) 1.34–35.

[66] Ibid., 48–50.

[67] Ernst Troeltsch, "Modern Philosophy of History" (1904), trans. James Luther Adams and Walter F. Bense in *Selected Essays of Ernst Troeltsch*, unpublished manuscript, 49. Cf. Troeltsch, *Social Teachings*, 2.1004.

[68] Troeltsch, "Modern Philosophy of History," 46–47. This work is largely a reflection on Heinrich Rickert's *The Limits of Concept Formation of the Natural Sciences: A Logical Introduction to the Historical Disciplines* (1903).

envisions as the didactic power of history in general and historic Christianity
in particular. Troeltsch speaks of supra-empirical typologies which grow out
of the inner productive power and in turn generate historical concepts.[69] It
remains to be seen, however, whether the apparent differences between
Troeltsch and Case are simply ones of garb, philosophical versus sociological,
or whether this initial discrepancy betokens a substantive disagreement.

Formgeschichte

In recent years it has been suggested by some scholars that Case's New
Testament work parallels or even anticipates the approach of the German
formgeschichtliche Schule.[70] Quite recently he has even been hailed as anticipating redaction criticism.[71] In part this discussion resembles an earlier
debate which took place at the time of Case's death and is reflected in C. C.
McCown's article in the Case commemorative issue of *The Journal of Religion* in 1949.[72]

Members of the Chicago School, especially members of the New Testament Department, were generally quite interested in the development of
the *formgeschichtliche* method. Case first formally discusses this approach
in 1925 when reviewing Erich Fascher's doctoral dissertation, *Die formgeschichtliche Methode*, in *The Journal of Religion*.[73] Both in this review and
in an article in the following issue, entitled "The Life of Jesus During the
Last Quarter-Century," Case displays an awareness of both the pertinent
literature and the basic positions espoused by the leading members of this
German school.

Prior to 1925, Case had already reviewed a number of the works of
individuals in this group. Thus in 1911 he had reviewed Rudolf Bultmann's
Der Stil der Paulinischen Predigt und die kynisch-stoische Diatribe, and
Johannes Weiss' *Die Aufgaben der neutestamentlichen Wissenschaft in der
Gegenwart*.[74] Various volumes of Weiss's *Das Urchristentum* were reviewed
by him between 1914 and 1921. Since Hermann Gunkel's works lay in the
Old Testament field, it is understandable that Case did not review any of

---

[69] Troeltsch, "Modern Philosophy of History," 31. See also Ernst Troeltsch, "What Does 'Essence of Christianity' Mean?" trans. Robert Morgan and Michael Pye, in *Ernst Troeltsch: Writings On Theology & Religion* (Atlanta: John Knox Press, 1977) 13, 23, 67.

[70] Coert Rylaarsdam views the relationship as parallel development. Cf. Coert Rylaarsdam,
"The Chicago School—And After," in *Transition in Biblical Studies*, ed. C. Rylaarsdam (Chicago: University of Chicago Press, 1968) 7. John Knox has suggested that the relationship is one
of anticipation on Case's part. Cf. John Knox, "Memories," 26.

[71] Funk, "Shirley Jackson Case," 9.

[72] McCown, "Shirley Jackson Case's Contributions," 30–47.

[73] Case, Review of Fascher's *Methode*, 428–31. S. J. Case, "The Life of Jesus During the Last
Quarter-Century," *The Journal of Religion* 5 (1925) 561–75.

[74] S. J. Case, Review of R. Bultmann's *Der Stil der Paulinischen Predigt und die kynisch-
stoische Diatribe* and J. Weiss' *Die Aufgaben der neutestamentlichen Wissenschaft in der
Gegenwart* in *The American Journal of Theology* 15 (1911) 286–89.

these works, although he frequently makes reference to them in his
Evolution.[75] While he was in editorial correspondence with Martin Dibelius
in 1931, Case did not review any of this author's works until 1940.[76]

As editor of *The Journal of Religion*, Case had corresponded with Bultmann about the possibility of an article for the journal on the new method
of *Formgeschichte*. This was probably in late 1925 or early 1926. Unfortunately, the copies of the correspondence have been removed at some time in
the past from the editorial files of *The Journal of Religion*. Only the empty
file, marked "Bultmann," remains.[77] The correspondence was evidently successful, however, as an article by Bultmann appeared in July 1926 entitled
"The New Approach to the Synoptic Problem."[78]

The editorial correspondence of this journal during this period gives
ample witness to the interest which Case had in this area. The following
year he attempted to solicit an article from Professor Charles Guignebert of
the Sorbonne on recent French interest in Jesus.[79] At the same time, he was
in contact with Professor Ludwig Köhler of the University of Zurich:

> I have just read with much interest your lecture on Das formgeschichtliche
> Problem des Neuen Testaments. I wish to procure for publication in the
> Journal of Religion an article along this line of investigation. In July, 1926,
> we published an article by Professor Bultmann on "The New Approach to
> the Synoptic Problem." In this he set forth the method of the *Formgeschicht-
> liche School* [*sic*]. I want to secure a criticism of the school in an article
> which might bear the title *A Critical Evaluation of Formgeschichte*. I have
> in mind a discussion of approximately eight thousand words, for which upon
> publication we can pay the sum of twenty-five dollars.[80]

Köhler's response to this inquiry was favorable and his article appeared in
October 1928 as "The Meaning and Possibilities of Formgeschichte."[81] Later,
Case also solicited from Martin Dibelius for a 1931 issue of *The Journal of
Religion* an article, which Case translated himself, entitled "Jesus in Con-
temporary German Theology."[82]

---

[75] Case, *Evolution*, 108, 128, 155, 193, 310, 349.

[76] S. J. Case, Review of M. Dibelius' *The Message of Jesus Christ* in *Religion in the Making*
1 (1940) 129–30.

[77] University of Chicago Archives, *The Journal of Religion* Letter File.

[78] Rudolf Bultmann, "The New Approach to the Synoptic Problem," *The Journal of Religion*
6 (1926) 337–62.

[79] Letter, S. J. Case to Charles Guignebert, October 27, 1927, University of Chicago Archives,
The Journal of Religion Letter File.

[80] Letter, S. J. Case to Ludwig Köhler, August 30, 1927, University of Chicago Archives, *The
Journal of Religion* Letter File.

[81] Ludwig Köhler, "The Meaning and Possibilities of Formgeschichte," *The Journal of Religion* 8 (1928) 603–15.

[82] Martin Dibelius, "Jesus in Contemporary German Theology," *The Journal of Religion* 11
(1931) 179–211. In 1940, Case's successor as Dean of the Divinity School, E. C. Colwell,

In 1927, Case drew a number of comparisons between *Formgeschichte* and some contemporary American scholarship in an extended footnote in his *Jesus*:

> More than a decade ago E. W. Parsons (*A Historical Examination of Some Non-Markan Elements in Luke* [Chicago, 1914]) explained the rise of certain sections in the gospel by reference to "problem-situations" in the life of the Christians. By such study he endeavored to fix the probable date and place at which selected portions of tradition arose. He was not concerned, however, with its specific literary forms. C. W. Votaw ("The Gospels and Contemporary Biographies," *The American Journal of Theology*, XIX [1915], 45–73, 217–249) examined the gospels beside other biographical literature of the age but did not carry the discussion into the field of origins. This phase of research has been pursued with especial vigor in Germany, where it is known as *Formgeschichte*. Its first exponents were K. L. Schmidt (*Der Rahmen der Geschichte Jesu* [Berlin, 1919]), who sought to demonstrate that the tradition incorporated in the gospels was originally devoid of any chronological and topographical scheme of unification; and M. Dibelius (*Formgeschichte des Evangeliums* [Tübingen, 1919]), who attempted a classification of different forms of early tradition as shaped by the practical needs of the Christian communities. This tradition was found to be the work of unliterary men who framed unconnected narratives—paradigms, short stories, apothegms, exhortations, legends—in accordance with the immediate necessities of their cult-life and missionary propaganda. R. Bultmann (*Die Geschichte der synoptischen Tradition* [Göttingen, 1921]) made his point of departure not the life-situations with the Christian society but the specific types of different units discoverable in the present gospel books. The result was the differentiation of distinctive forms not essentially dissimilar to those specified by Dibelius.[83]

Although Case links these American approaches with those of the German *Formgeschichte* group, he does not explicitly include his own socio-historical method. It could be argued that when this footnote is placed within the context of that portion of *Jesus* to which it is appended, then the socio-historical method is implicitly included in the discussion. However, C. C. McCown's interpretation that Case explicitly included himself in this passage is inaccurate.[84]

This footnote is fundamentally a critical comparison of somewhat similar methods. Thus, while pointing out the similarity between *Formgeschichte* and Parsons' method of matching Gospel passages to particular "problem

---

attempted to have Dibelius accept a temporary appointment at the Divinity School: "I still have some hopes of adding a distinguished scholar, such as M. Dibelius, to the staff. I have written a letter to him sounding him out. . . ." Letter, E. C. Colwell to Edgar J. Goodspeed, September 4, 1940, University of Chicago Archives, Goodspeed Letter File.

[83] Case, *Jesus* 102–4, n. 1. This footnote, abnormally long by Case's standards, goes on to furnish a detailed international bibliography of works employing *Formgeschichte*.

[84] McCown, "Shirley Jackson Case's Contribution," 25. "Case . . . calls attention to the fact that he . . . had anticipated the German form-history by several years."

situations" in the Christian community, Case notes at the same time that Parsons was unconcerned with specific literary forms.[85] Beyond such critical comparisons, this passage is not intent on making any claims of chronological anticipation or competitive claims of "who got there first."

Within the text of *Jesus*, this comparison focuses upon the relative adequacy of these methods. At this point Case distinguishes two basic approaches to biblical criticism, the historical-literary and the historical-social, as has already been discussed in Chapter III. In this treatment, Case does not explicitly speak of *Formgeschichte*, as he had done in the appended footnote, but rather of the "new school."[86] For Case, the historical-social types of criticism form a continuum. Thus, tests of literary genre or internal laws of literary development must at some point be linked to the social situations in which they were formed. While all higher criticism must begin with the literary issues, the more adequate higher criticism will include the social test as well.

In 1925, Case defined the aim of the *formgeschichtliche* approach as seeking "to determine the historical process that gave fixity to the oral tradition as it passed into literary form, a process determined more by the use of the material in the cult life of the communities than by the literary skill of any individual authors."[87] This definition, when fitted into the two types of criticism set out in 1927 in *Jesus*, would seem to indicate again that optimal *Formgeschichte* does not stop with mere *Literaturgeschichte* but goes beyond to the social setting. By implication, Case would seem to place both this socially-oriented type of *Formgeschichte* and his own socio-historical method in this second type of criticism, the historical-social.

The above explicit and implicit comparisons represent the closest Case ever seems to have come to speaking definitively to the question of what relationship might have existed between *Formgeschichte* and the socio-historical method. Beyond this, there are a number of significant thematic parallels between the two methods.

For example, both methods employ the technique of literary forms and the test of the relationship to the social environment. With respect to the former, it is not entirely accurate to say that Case practiced "form criticism without the forms," since he did in fact use literary forms briefly in *Jesus*. Still, it is fair to say that these forms were never used as consistently and

---

[85] This critique of Parsons by Case is not unlike Colwell's later analysis of Case that he practiced "form criticism without the forms." As quoted by Funk in "Shirley Jackson Case," 8.

[86] Case, *Jesus*, 103ff. See Chapter III, 44.

[87] Case, Review of Fascher's *Methode* 430–31. This same view of *Formgeschichte* as encompassing both the historical-literary and the historical-social types of criticism is shared by Case's colleagues, Harold Willoughby and Donald Riddle. Cf. Harold Willoughby, "The Study of Early Christianity During the Last Quarter-Century," *The Journal of Religion* 6 (1926) 280ff. Cf. Donald Riddle, *Jesus and the Pharisees* (Chicago: University of Chicago Press, 1928) 4, 94, 173–78.

thoroughly by Case as they were by members of the *Formgeschichte* group. The primary stress of the socio-historical method is upon the social environment rather than upon literary forms. Therein lies a significant difference of emphasis between the two methods.

This difference with regard to literary forms might also be described by observing that Case was not so much engaged in *Formgeschichte* as in what might be called *Themengeschichte*. Thus, while Bultmann and Case reach similar conclusions about both miracle stories and the figure of Christ as miracle worker, Bultmann does this by extensive comparison of the literary structure of Hellenistic miracle stories and miracles in the Scriptures. Case reaches his conclusions more by a consideration of the general literary theme of miraculous happenings within Hellenistic and Judaic society.

With respect to the predominance of the social stress in the socio-historical method, John Knox has suggested that this stress to some extent anticipates *Formgeschichte*:

> Before the form critics had their present vogue, and quite independently of their influence, he [Case] was forcing us to look *through* the ancient documents of the New Testament to the ancient life reflected in them and forcing us also to see this life in the most realistic way possible for us. I do not recall his using the phrase *Sitz im Leben*, but no one was ever more insistent on the necessity of the interpreter's knowing it.[88]

Between Case and members of the *Formgeschichte* tradition there are a number of interesting thematic similarities and differences. With respect to Bultmann and Case in particular, there are not only several thematic parallels but some limited biographical parallels as well. Having studied at Marburg University during the first decade of this century, both probably worked under the same teachers in some instances. Thus, it is highly probable that each had studied under Adolf Jülicher, whose writings receive favorable mention by both. Accordingly, Case would have been aware of Jülicher's two volume *Die Gleichnisreden Jesu* (1889), which Bultmann regards as precedential with respect to *Formgeschichte*.[89]

Case would agree with both Bultmann and Martin Kähler that there is a valid distinction between the historical Jesus and the Christ of the gospels. In addition, as previously indicated, he would share their criticism of the liberal *Leben-Jesu-Forschung* as continually recasting Jesus in the changing colors of an ever-shifting liberal portrait. However, on the significant issue of

---

[88] Knox, "Memories," 26. The anticipation here claimed seems to be on the order of temporal precedence and in itself does not seem to be linked with causal influence. Knox does not fall victim to the logical fallacy of *post hoc propter hoc*.

[89] Bultmann, "New Approach," 354, 360. Case and Bultmann viewed their own respective methods as growing out of the earlier *Religionsgeschichte* approach.

whether or not a life of Jesus could be written from the gospels, Case and
Bultmann would part company. For Bultmann, *Formgeschichte* comes

> to the negative conclusion that the outline of the Gospels does not enable us
> to know either the outer course of the life of Jesus or his inner development.
> We must frankly confess that the character of Jesus as a human personality
> cannot be recovered by us. We can neither write a "life of Jesus" nor present
> an accurate picture of his personality.[90]

Obviously Case would hold the contrary position. In this, some might place
him closer to the later "New Quest" of various post-Bultmannians, that is, providing for some actual continuity between the historical Jesus and the Christ
of faith.[91] At least one analysis would place B. W. Bacon, Case's teacher at
Yale, in the same group as anticipating the post-Bultmannian concerns.[92]

On the surface it might seem that Case would be in fundamental disagreement with both Bultmann and Kähler with respect to the object of faith being
the Christ of the kerygma rather than the historical Jesus. Although Case is in
search of the personal religion of the historical Jesus rather than the Christ of
the kerygma, neither of these can be considered normative. Nevertheless,
Bultmann's kerygma and Case's religion of Jesus seem to operate in somewhat
similar ways. The former serves as the confrontation point for the believer
with Christ; the latter serves as a didactic encounter between the believer and
the basic spiritual consciousness of the historical Jesus.[93]

With respect to the assessment of the relationship between Case's socio-
historical method and *Formgeschichte*, one scholar is particularly notable
for his accurate and judicious analysis of this relationship over a period of

---

[90] Ibid., 359.

[91] Ernst Käsemann, "Das Problem des historischen Jesus," *Zeitschrift für Theologie und
Kirche* 51 (1954) 125–53.

[92] Roy A. Harrisville, "Representative American Lives of Jesus," in *The Historical Jesus and
the Kerygmatic Christ* by Carl E. Braaten and Roy A. Harrisville (New York: Abingdon Press,
1964) 186. The major point of anticipation is "the inseparability for the Christian faith of the
'Gospel of Jesus' from the 'Gospel about Jesus.'" This is of course a central distinction for
Bacon's pupil, S. J. Case. By the same token, there are a number of interesting thematic similarities between Case and the "New Hermeneutic" of Ernst Fuchs and Gerhard Ebeling, e.g., the
parallel between the message of Jesus and the message about Jesus, the affirmation that the
message necessarily involves the messenger, and the conviction that knowledge of the historical
Jesus may be used to interpret the kerygma. For a discussion of these matters, see Norman
Perrin, "The Challenge of New Testament Theology Today," *Criterion* 4 (1965) 25ff.

[93] Like most members of the Chicago School, Case had little use for the Barthian theology
which he found in Bultmann's *Jesus and the Word*. In reviewing this work, Case observed that
Bultmann modernized and idealized the historical Jesus as much as any Ritschlian liberal, except that now Jesus was modernized "by portraying him as an exponent of Barthian theology."
Case scores both Barth and Bultmann for their unconcern with the life and personality of Jesus,
as seen in their view that Jesus' message was "from without and not an expression of ideals and
attainments inherent in his own spiritual personality." S. J. Case, Review of Rudolf Bultmann's
Jesus and the Word in *The Journal of Religion* 15 (1935) 84–85.

decades. He was Henry J. Cadbury, recently deceased, Professor Emeritus of Harvard Divinity School and recipient of the Nobel Peace Prize. In addition to his own expertise in the New Testament field, he was especially qualified to speak to this issue because of his long and thorough familiarity with both methods from their initiation onwards. Thus, Cadbury was one of the first American scholars, if not the first, to have called attention to the new *Formgeschichte* School within his article, "Between Jesus and the Gospels," in the *Harvard Theological Review* in 1923.[94] The following year, he reviewed the Gunkel Festschrift which contained essays by Bultmann, Dibelius and other leading *Formgeschichte* figures.[95] It was to Cadbury that Case, as editor of *The Journal of Religion*, turned for a review of his own *Jesus* in 1928. Since such a review involved the editor's own work, Case delicately counseled Cadbury that all that was necessary was "a plain statement of judgment."[96] In accepting the review task, Cadbury replied that he would review this work as any other: "Those who know us both know that we are not bound by any special academic or theological strings. I am not a member of the 'Chicago school of thought.'"[97]

In his review, Cadbury commented:

> There has been developing a new school of criticism at Chicago. In this volume we have a chance to hear the technique expounded and to see it at work. How does it commend itself to us? In theory it is of course quite sound, but it is not perhaps so new in biblical study as its advocates fancy. The gospels have long been understood as palimpsests in which the original facts are covered by later interpretation. Founders of schools of criticism often seem newer than they are.[98]

Several months later, Cadbury commented for the first time on the parallelism between the socio-historical method and *Formgeschichte*:

> The student of the gospel wishes, however, some not too subjective norm for testing the accuracy of the gospel items. Form criticism claimed to supply such a standard. And the form critics freely expressed their judgments. Their

---

[94] Henry J. Cadbury, "Between Jesus and the Gospels," *Harvard Theological Review* 16 (1923) 81–92.

[95] Henry J. Cadbury, Review of *Festschrift für Hermann Gunkel* in *Harvard Theological Review* 17 (1923) 303–6.

[96] Letter, S. J. Case to Henry J. Cadbury, August 8, 1927, University of Chicago Archives, *The Journal of Religion* Letter File.

[97] Letter, Henry J. Cadbury to S. J. Case, August 11, 1927, University of Chicago Archives, *The Journal of Religion* Letter File.

[98] Henry J. Cadbury, Review of *Jesus: A New Biography*, in *The Journal of Religion* 8 (1928) 132. This criticism was quite similar to one which Cadbury had already applied to form critics: "Like all innovators, the 'formgeschichtliche' are in danger of over exalting their tools or techniques, like one who 'sacrifices unto his net and burns incense unto his drag.'" Cf. Cadbury, Review of *Festschrift für Hermann Gunkel*, 305.

> method coincided closely with Professor Case's technique of "criticism by
> social environment." What was capable of explanations suiting the viewpoint
> of the later Christians was regarded as unauthentic. Though he does not
> mention Professor Case's *Jesus* in the study of "the synoptic perspective,"
> Professor Easton [in his *The Gospel Before the Gospels*], in answering the
> skeptical radicalism of Bultman [*sic*] is equally answering the Chicago
> professor.[99]

Some thirty years later, writing in retrospect about the New Testament
scholarship of the preceding half century, Cadbury made this comparison
more explicit. "Form criticism began in Germany about the end of the First
World War; demythologizing about the end of the Second. The Chicago
school's emphasis on 'environmental factors' was an independent parallel to
form criticism."[100] In correspondence just prior to his death, Cadbury further
specified his judgment on the chronology of these movements: "Case's approach was earlier than and not due to form criticism, which first was
known in America about 1923."[101]

This assertation about chronology, when added to Knox's earlier comment about *Sitz im Leben*, opens up an interesting question, if one lying beyond the limited scope of this chapter. Exploration of anticipation would
have to involve a determination of the precise time that each method or the
key elements in each method came into conceptual and literary existence,
and at what time the respective methods began to be known by others on a
national or international level. Careful attention would also have to be given
to distinguishing between anticipation, in the sense of temporal precedence,
and demonstrable causal influence. Otherwise, discussions of anticipation
could all too easily fall victim to the logical fallacy of *post hoc propter hoc*
already mentioned.

For the moment, however what has gone before seems to indicate clearly that Case shares several similar methodological perspectives with *Formgeschichte*. On the other hand, the respective chronologies of *Formgeschichte*
and Case's own socio-historical method would seem to support Cadbury's
contention that the latter is an independent but parallel development in
relation to the former. Finally, it must be reemphasized that if Case's awareness of this German movement was carefully cultivated, it was nonetheless a
notably critical awareness. Case is quite outspoken in what he perceives as
the inadequacy of each of the individual advocates of *Formgeschichte* as
well as of the method taken as a whole, and he suggests repeatedly that his
own socio-historical method is a means of transcending these inadequacies.

---

[99] Henry J. Cadbury, Review of Burton Scott Easton's *The Gospel Before the Gospels*, in
The Journal of Religion 8 (1928) 629.

[100] Henry J. Cadbury, "Fifty Years of New Testament Scholarship," *Journal of Bible & Religion* 28 (1960) 194.

[101] Letter, Henry J. Cadbury to William J. Hynes, July 4, 1970.

Conclusion: Possible German Influences

At the onset of the present treatment of possible German influences upon the socio-historical method of S. J. Case, two major sets of opinions were mentioned. The first viewed this relationship as one of outright parenthood with the older German scholars begetting their younger American counterparts. The second stressed the independence of the socio-historical method.

Indeed some evidence of direct intellectual parenthood has been seen both in Foster's use of Troeltsch and the Neo-Kantians as well as in the acknowledged Ritschlianism of Case and Smith. Nonetheless, both Case and Smith sought to move beyond their earlier Ritschlianism as they began to perceive serious weaknesses inherent within it. In the end, the evidence examined would seem to indicate that the relationship between German scholarship and Case's thought was definitely neither one of simple genetic parenthood nor one of uninformed independence.

Not content merely to have studied briefly at the centers of German scholarship, Case and many of his colleagues were intent on continually updating their own awareness of German developments as clearly evidenced in their own publications, lecture series and personal correspondence. There is certainly little question that these German groups did provide the general scholarly horizon against which many of the Chicago School members worked during this period. However, even where noteworthy thematic parallels and similarities exist between the two groups, there are at the same time equally significant thematic differences or variations.

In short, for most members of the Chicago School, particularly for Case and his socio-historical method, this relationship is neither one of determinative dependence nor naive ignorance but rather one of informed independence.

Possible American Influences

Introduction

If German theological scholarship provided the horizon against which many Chicago School figures measured the stature and worth of their own work, it is also true that the foreground through which this work was focused was provided by American intellectual scholarship and social milieu. In terms of possible originating influences on the American scene, two specific areas need to be considered. They are the relation of the socio-historical method to the Yale School and to American pragmatism.

The Yale School: B. W. Bacon and F. C. Porter

Long before S. J. Case arrived at Chicago, a significant tie existed between the Divinity Schools of the University of Chicago and Yale University. It was at Yale that William Rainey Harper received his doctorate prior to joining, in 1878, the faculty of the forerunner of the Divinity School of the University of Chicago, the Baptist Union Theological Seminary in Morgan Park, Illinois, to teach Hebrew. It was back to Yale that he subsequently returned in order to accept a similar position there.[102] While at Yale this time, Harper engaged in the negotiations with John D. Rockefeller which resulted in the founding of the new University of Chicago with Harper as President. These initial ties to Yale at one point resulted in Harper's being depreciatingly characterized as a "Yale rationalist."[103]

Case received all three of his graduate degrees from Yale Divinity School between 1901 and 1907. He was an instructor in the Divinity School at the time he left Yale. In later reflection, Case distinguished three major periods within the history of the Yale Divinity School: (1) from 1822 to 1860—the period of N. W. Taylor, T. W. Gibbs, Fitsch, and Goodrich, (2) from 1860 to 1895—the period of P. Schaff, G. B. Stevens, and Curtis and (3) from 1895 to 1922—the period of F. C. Porter, B. W. Bacon, and Williston Walker.[104] It is this last period of Porter and Bacon, under whom Case had studied, of which Case spoke so eloquently, as we have already seen:

> Under such men, New Testament studies at Yale represented a position considerably in advance of that which prevailed at the English and Scottish universities and more in line with the work that was being carried on in Germany by, for example, Jülicher and the older Holtzmann. But this thorough acquaintance with world scholarship never degenerated into a mere echo of foreign opinions. When the biblical teachers at Yale spoke, it was to express conviction of their own, that had been reached in the full light of opinions held by their own predecessors and contemporaries, but that represented in every instance a careful criticism and reworking of the materials and problems involved, or a piece of further investigation in some new section of the field.[105]

Although Case never discussed what he might have specifically inherited from Porter or Bacon, it is obvious from the above quote as well as the Festschrift which Case edited in honor of Porter and Bacon, *Studies in Early Christianity* (1928), that Case prized highly the work of his teachers.[106] In conjunction with an earlier discussion of this quote, it was

---

[102] According to Shailer Mathews, Harper did not merely have *a* position at Yale but in fact held three different chairs at the same time. Mathews, *New Faith for Old*, 61. In his first work on the Chicago School, Harvey Arnold credits Harper with holding two chairs at the same time. Arnold, *Near the Edge of Battle*, 6. However, in a more recent work, Arnold has increased this figure to agree with Mathews. See Arnold, *God Before You and Behind You*, 149.

[103] Dr. Mendenhall in *The Christian Advocate* (1889), as quoted by Funk, "Watershed," 8.

[104] Case, "Contributions of the Yale Divinity School," 19–24.

[105] Ibid., 23.

[106] S. J. Case, ed., *Studies in Early Christianity* (New York: Century Co., 1928) i–ix.

suggested that not only did Case value this attitude of informed independence in his teachers, but also he attempted to imbue his own work with the same attitude.[107]

There are a number of interesting thematic similarities between the work of these two Yale professors and that of their student. All three figures were deeply dedicated to use of the critical historical method in the study of matters religious.[108] Methodologically, however, Case's socio-historical method would seem closer to Bacon's "aetiological method" than to Porter's "appreciative method."

Porter's method places central stress upon the subjective or poetic quality of an interpreter to regain the past through imaginative identification with it. Roy Harrisville comments that for Porter this work of the imagination must take precedence over historical research.[109] Even though Case's work is not without its creative use of the imagination, particularly in recovering the experience of specific historical individuals, his dedication to sober historical and scientific research would not allow his subscription to this formal methodological preference.

In this latter vein, however, Porter and Case do mutually subscribe to the scientific canon of interpretation which prefers "that which can be repeated in our experience and not some unique event which by its very nature is incapable of repetition and therefore of verification."[110] In the use of this test, both scholars operate within the tradition of David Hume's critique of miracles. Case's use of this test is somewhat more sweeping than Porter's. Thus the latter is overtly reluctant to apply this canon to the divinity of Jesus, preferring to switch to the experience of the renewing power of Jesus as the primary method of verification. Case, however, never found it necessary to restrict explicitly the application of this canon to the divinity of Jesus. This may stem from his greater concern to stress both the historicity and personal religion of Jesus.

With regard to the personal religion of Jesus, both men generally maintain the standard Ritschlian position that while not all the details of Jesus' life are available, still the total impression of his life and character is recoverable.[111] Both Case and Porter were interested in the power of Jesus' personality and the ability of his religion to generate faith in others. Thus for Porter, "the greatness of Jesus and his secret and his divinity . . . is most nearly disclosed in the power that he had to produce in men a living faith that was not bound to his earthly presence . . . words . . . and the life he

---

[107] See above, 102ff.

[108] Case, "Contributions of the Yale Divinity School," 22–23.

[109] Roy A. Harrisville, *Frank Chamberlain Porter: Pioneer in American Biblical Interpretation* (Missoula, Montana: Scholars Press, 1976) 13ff.

[110] Roland Bainton, *Yale and the Ministry* (New York: Harper & Row, 1967) 221.

[111] F. C. Porter, "Inquiries Concerning the Divinity of Jesus," *The American Journal of Theology* 8 (1904) 24.

lived."[112] In Case's writings, however, this generative power is never tied so explicitly to the divinity of Jesus.

With respect to the necessity of the historicity of Jesus in the above equation, Case and Porter differ significantly. For Porter, the renewing power of Jesus could exist even if Jesus had never lived.[113] For Case, on the other hand, the existence and reality of the personal religion of Jesus is fundamentally dependent upon the actual historical existence of Jesus. At this point, Case would appear to be closer to Bacon than to Porter. As has already been noted, both Bacon and Case maintained the inseparability of the Gospel of Jesus and the Gospel about Jesus.[114]

Bacon is critical of the "liberal Christ" as a "cause utterly inadequate to account for the rise of the religion" of Christianity.[115] Similarly Case levels criticisms against various liberal presumptions, especially the retrospective projection that the "essence" of contemporary Christianity equals the "essence" of early Christianity.[116]

With regard to Bacon's and Case's mutual interest in the application of a critical historical method to the study of religion, both were deeply appreciative of the approach of the *religionsgeschichtliche Schule*. Thus, Bacon, speaking at the Fifth World Congress for Free Christianity and Religious Progress in Berlin in 1910, called for a genetic study of Christian ideas from the viewpoint of *Religionsgeschichte*.[117] This substantially represents what Bacon was doing within his own aetiological method, that is, attempting to understand the New Testament in terms of the ongoing life and controversies of the early Christian community.[118] In the end, however, Bacon's aetiological method focuses more strongly upon literary motives, whereas Case's socio-historical method seeks to move beyond this to the external social settings. Further Bacon is quite intrigued with the triads of Hegel, something for which Case has absolutely no taste.

Most secondary sources are silent about the possible influence of either Bacon or Porter upon Case's socio-historical method. Thus, while David Riddle already in 1928 saw Bacon's work as preceding *Formgeschichte*, he

---

[112] Ibid., 18.

[113] Bainton, *Yale and the Ministry*, 225.

[114] See below, 120–22.

[115] B. W. Bacon, "The Teaching Ministry for Tomorrow," *The Centennial Celebration of the Founding of the Yale Divinity School*, 14.

[116] See Chapter II, 20–21.

[117] B. W. Bacon, *Die Ergebnisse der Bibelkritik für Theologie und Praxis* (Berlin-Schoneberg: Protestantischer Schriftenvertrieb, 1911), as cited by Harrisville, "Representative American Lives of Jesus," 186. Since Case was in Germany during this same year and in Berlin at least on one occasion, one may wonder if he was able to be in attendance for Bacon's address.

[118] B. W. Bacon, "Ultimate Problems of Biblical Science," *Journal of Biblical Literature* 22 (1903) 1–14. For a discussion of the similarities between Bacon and F. C. Baur, see Harrisville, *Porter*, 103ff.

does not comment upon Bacon's possible influence upon Case.[119] One of the first comments upon this relationship comes from Robert Funk who briefly remarks that Case "appears to have put greater stock in the historical method than either of his teachers" at Yale.[120] Roy Harrisville has recently commented that "Bacon's 'aetiological criticism' is a dead ringer for what currently passes for *Formgeschichte*, and that Bacon and no one else was responsible for its introduction to this country, if not for its actual invention." However, with respect to the relationship between Bacon's and Case's respective methods, Harrisville does not deal explicitly with this but nevertheless implies a strong influence of the aetiological method upon the socio-historical method.[121] For Case's part when he discusses *Formgeschichte* and its American parallels, he does not mention either Bacon or Porter.[122]

While there are thematic similarities between Case's work and that of his two teachers, in the end his work seems closer to that of Bacon than that of Porter. There are significant similarities between Bacon's aetiological method and aspects within the socio-historical method such as the historical factor and the genetic factor; nonetheless, there are also aspects within the latter method not present in the former such as the didactic factor, the vitalistic factor and so on.

Given these thematic similarities as well as the fact of Case's extended graduate work under both teachers at Yale, and notwithstanding Case's lack of explicit commentary on either figure as a possible source of influence upon him, the probability of some influence, especially by Bacon, is reasonably high. However, this relationship is again not one of uncritical dependence but more one of critical and independent appropriation.

American Pragmatism

Some of the thought of the Chicago School, including the socio-historical method, has been characterized as pragmatic in nature and occasionally linked with leading figures of American pragmatism, such as William James and John Dewey. For example, H. J. Cadbury, in reviewing Case's *Jesus*, remarked that Case "sounded like William James."[123]

Having just seen the thoroughgoing awareness and scholarly discussions in which Case and others in the Chicago School participated with respect to German theological developments, one might justifiably expect to find an equally thorough discussion of the central figures in American pragmatism, especially considering the contemporaneous presence of John Dewey and

---

[119] Riddle, *Jesus and the Pharisees*, 93–94.

[120] Funk, "Watershed," 15.

[121] Roy A. Harrisville, *Benjamin Wisner Bacon: Pioneer in American Biblical Criticism* (Missoula, MT: Scholars Press, 1976) iv. Contrast this with Harrisville's earlier position in "Representative Lives of Jesus," 186.

[122] Case, *Jesus*, 102–4, n. 1.

[123] Cadbury, Review of S. J. Case's *Jesus*, 134.

George Herbert Mead at the University of Chicago. Accordingly, it is somewhat startling to find a virtual absence of such discussion in either the work
of Case or Matthews. To find this discussion, one must look to the more
declaredly philosophically inclined, such as G. B. Foster, Foster's disciple A.
Eustace Haydon, William Scribner Ames in philosophy, or much later,
Henry Nelson Wieman.

For his part, Case neither reviews any of the writings of the American
pragmatists nor does he pen any major work on this topic as such. During
the three decades during which *The American Journal of Theology* was in
existence, there were only three reviews of James' works and only a single
review of a work by Dewey.[124] When extended discussions of pragmatism do
occur in this journal, they are to be found within such articles as Ames'
"Theology from the Standpoint of Functional Psychology" (1906), Foster's
"Pragmatism and Knowledge," (1907), and Haydon's "The Theological
Trend of Pragmatism" (1919).[125] There are also several articles by non-
Chicago figures in this area, such as Arthur D. Lovejoy's "Pragmatism and
Theology" (1908) and Anne Louis Strong's "Some Religious Aspects of Prag-
matism" (1908).[126]

This lack of any direct concern with American pragmatism on the part of
Mathews and Case may be but a smaller part of the larger anti-metaphysical
and anti-philosophical bias associated both with their earlier Ritschlianism
and with their later socio-historical method. Both Case and Mathews seem to
prefer that philosophical questions be bracketed with respect to Christianity
and theological methods. Accordingly, for Mathews the type of positive
method necessary for developing an evangelical theology should be "non-
metaphysical, non-epistemological" in character.[127] Further, Mathews is far
more willing than Case to enter these brackets temporarily to state that the
essence of Christianity contains metaphysical elements. Nonetheless, the
question arises for both men as to when such brackets might be removed so

---

[124] D. C. MacIntosh reviewed William James' *Pragmatism: A New Name for Some Old
Ways of Thinking*, in *The American Journal of Theology* 12 (1908) 162–67. George B. Stevens
of Yale reviewed William James' *The Variety of Religious Experience*, in *The American
Journal of Theology* 7 (1903) 114–17. James Seth reviewed William James' *The Will to
Believe*, in *The American Journal of Theology* 15 (1911) 142–46. The only work of Dewey
which was ever reviewed in this journal was a book which he coauthored, entitled *Ethics*, in
The American Journal of Theology 13 (1909) 140–43.

[125] Edward Scribner Ames, "Theology From the Standpoint of Functional Psychology," *The
American Journal of Theology* 10 (1906) 219–32. George Burman Foster, "Pragmatism and
Knowledge," *The American Journal of Theology* 11 (1907) 591–96. A. Eustace Haydon, "The
Theological Trends of Pragmatism," *The American Journal of Theology* 23 (1919) 401–16.

[126] Arthur D. Lovejoy, "Pragmatism and Theology," *The American Journal of Theology* 12
(1908) 116–143. Anne Louis Strong, "Some Religious Aspects of Pragmatism," *The American
Journal of Theology* 12 (1908) 231–48.

[127] Cf. Shailer Mathews, "A Positive Method for an Evangelical Theology," *The American
Journal of Theology* 13 (1909) 21–46.

that philosophical considerations could prevail. While we might infer from Case's silence that such considerations are always inappropriate, Mathews seems open to such activity in theory but is suspicious of the ability of philosophers to practice their trade constructively within these brackets.

Not only were Case and Mathews virtually uninterested in pursuing underlying questions of philosophical or cosmic truth, but also these concerns for Mathews bordered on being antithetical to church membership. He sees G. B. Foster as a prime illustration of this:

> Professor Foster was a good representative of the movement in thought which was increasingly removed from the perception that Christianity is a religious movement rather than merely a system of truths. The importance of non-church-going religious philosophers is great but their influence is indirect if not negligible so far as operative Christianity is concerned. They find themselves increasingly out of sympathy with Christian groups and tend to dissociate themselves from organized religious work. The choice between an attitude and that of a continued participation in organized church life sooner or later has to be made.[128]

For Mathews, one must choose between viewing the Christian religion from a philosophical vantage point or participating "in the actual recasting of the Christian movement."[129] In short, the choice is between philosophy or evangelism; one excludes the other. When Foster persisted in pursuing issues of philosophical and cosmic truth as well as detailed applications of pragmatism and other philosophies to Christianity against the outraged cries of various church groups throughout the Midwest, Dean Burton and President Harper arranged to have Foster transferred into the Philosophy Department. Parallel ideological discussions by Ames, who was in the Philosophy Department from the start, seem to have presented little problem for either Burton or Mathews. Foster's disciple, A. Eustace Haydon, continued many of his mentor's pursuits but from within the Humanities as Professor of Comparative Religions.

This separatistic attitude within the Divinity School toward philosophy started to break down in the late 1920s. As has already been noted, G. B. Smith began to be interested in the question of cosmic support for human values as well as the philosophical issues implied in various theological methods. In both a symbolic and substantive sense, this split was bridged by the recruitment and appointment of the pro-philosophical Henry Nelson Wieman *within* the Divinity School as Professor of Christian Theology and Philosophy of Religion in 1927. According to Bernard Meland, the use of philosophical works such as those of William James, Henri Bergson and Alfred North Whitehead increased appreciably with the advent of Wieman

---

[128] Mathews, *New Faith for Old*, 69–70.
[129] Ibid., 70.

to the Divinity School faculty.[130] To a significant degree his coming may mark the beginning of a decline of the general suspicion of philosophy dominant since Foster's transfer. With Wieman, philosophical issues and particular philosophical systems, such as pragmatism and process thought, began to receive a degree of attention and discussion comparable to that already seen with respect to German scholarship.

Granting the lack of in-depth and explicit discussion of pragmatism by either Mathews or Case, within a general context of maintaining an antiphilosophical posture, two assertions by Meland in this area seem quite valid. The first and more general assertion is that the early Chicago School assimilated "a pragmatic cast of mind" which was part of the American mainstream.[131] The second and more specific assertion is that "the method of inquiry into the growth of religious ideas as practiced by the Chicago School frankly presupposes the philosophical orientation of pragmatism with its functional view of truth and ideas."[132] In both cases, philosophy is "bootlegged" in through the back door.[133]

Meland's first assertion is basically a variation of Frederick Jackson Turner's thesis applied to the Chicago School:

> The Chicago School of theology arose amidst the groundbreaking for a new and independent university in midwest America. This new University of Chicago, in turn, began taking form at the turn of the century within a prairie-land culture that was feeling its way into a distinctive mode of the American experience. The rise of the packing industry had been one of the major expressions of that new cultural experience through the latter half of the nineteenth century. Bold innovations in architecture by the young architect, Louis Sullivan, that would eventuate in the skyscraper in their way provided the artistic model and symbol for the leviathan culture then emerging, a functional art, a way of expressing beauty and feeling within the demands and necessities of the work-a-day world. A pragmatic temper of mind, born of necessity, and transmuted into an ideal and a way of life, was aborning in this wide expanse of prairie-land which was to be the home of the new university and its Divinity School.
>
> This pragmatic temper of mind was to be given formidable expression within the university in the person of John Dewey who, in 1898, became head of the Department of Philosophy, and later of the Department of Pedagogy as well, as the Department of Education was then called. Other areas of

---

[130] Meland, "Reflections on the Chicago School," 23. There is a special irony here since Wieman seems to have been the first Chicago figure since Foster to have been a serious student of the work of Ernst Troeltsch.

[131] Ibid., 2.

[132] Ibid., 19.

[133] Meland, Discussion Vanderbilt Conference.

the university, including the Divinity School, were to assimilate this pragmatic temper of mind and to make it their own.[134]

The obverse side of this pragmatic cast of mind involved severing ties with
the "genteel tradition" of Eastern America and Europe to some extent. A
notable example which would seem to corroborate this dynamic is the list of
regional cultural qualities which John Henry Adams drew up to help him
decide whether to continue to teach at Johns Hopkins University in Balti-
more or to accept the offer of an exceptionally well paid position at the new
University of Chicago:

Baltimore	*Chicago*
Quiet	Rush
Continuity	Broken
Experience	Experiment
Society	New People
Conservatism	Boom
Baltimore	*Chicago*
Duty	Advantage
Assured Position	All New
Settled	Moving
Identification	Lost[135]

This list, of course, helped convince Adams to stay in the middle of the
genteel tradition.

As has already been indicated, the individuals at Chicago were great
respecters of the genteel tradition particularly in its European guise. However, on occasion the process of updating one's own knowledge of German
scholarship could be placed in stark contrast with the equally valued pragmatic cast of mind. Thus, Wilhelm Pauck has recalled with great humor and
gusto several instances of such a contrast occasioned by the German scholars
responding to invitations to visit Chicago:

> They [the members of the Chicago School] felt themselves in alliance with
> the German theological scholars because of the historical method. . . . Other-
> wise . . . they were . . . concerned to be American and as such they wished
> to be different from the Germans and they didn't want to be dependent
> upon the Germans in any way. [Mathews] . . . despised learning for learning's
> sake. He suggested that much theological learning as it was displayed by the
> German theological scholars was irrelevant. Of course, one must say that the
> German professors and theologians often had a way of illustrating how irrele-
> vant their learning could be. . . . Eduard Meyer was certainly one of the
> most accomplished historians of . . . the whole ancient world. . . . He was

---

[134] Meland, "Reflections of the Chicago School," 2–3. Funk sees the formation of the Chicago
School as arising out of "a frontier mentality." Funk, "Shirley Jackson Case," 14.

[135] Richard Hofstadter, *The Progressive Historians* (New York: Vintage Books, 1968) 67.

invited to come to Chicago to lecture. Do you know what he chose to deal with? The duel! It just took the breath away from all these scholars! Then he undertook a trip through the United States and became most intrigued with the Mormons. Upon returning to Germany, he wrote a two volume history of the Mormons! . . . Gustav Krüger, a very accomplished historian of the ancient church, one of the first pupils of Harnack, and one of those to whom Case felt intellectually attached . . . came to Chicago. One would expect that he would deliver himself of his own speciality and support, you might say, his cause, as it was being furthered at Chicago. He went into the library during his first week of residence in the city and discovered that Chicago possessed one of the most remarkable collections of deist literature. And instead of lecturing on the ancient church, or methods of studying Christian antiquity, he lectured, drew up an entirely new course, on the deists! . . . Arthur Titius a few years later was invited, largely I believe, on the initiative of G. B. Smith. G. B. Smith was embarrassed in his own theological thinking as a Ritschlian because he really could not make sense of the relationship between religion . . . and science. . . . And so they invited Titius, an old time Ritschlian, a pupil of Julius Kaftan, who for several decades after the death of Ritschl had really ruled the Ritschlian roost in Germany. Titius in his mature years had turned to the study of the natural science; and just before he was asked to come to Chicago, he had published a huge tome entitled *Natur und Gott*, a very remarkable achievement. . . . He came to Chicago brim full of this learning, a Ritschlian acquainted with the whole strain of the natural sciences and all that pertained to them. What did he lecture on? The possibilities of an ecumenical theology! What was remarkable about this was the tolerance of these Chicago people! Nobody told Krüger: "Look, you don't know a thing about the history of the church during the 18th century, and we want you to deal with your scope of it." Nobody prohibited Titius from trying out his ideas on the ecumenical movement. This certainly made plain the truth of Mathews' idea that learning can be awfully irrelevant.[136]

It seems that the Chicago School was tolerant of the temporary suspension of the pragmatic concerns of their foreground in service to the process, if not always the reality, of updating their awareness of the German horizon.

Meland's second more specific assertion is that the method of the Chicago School "presupposes the philosophical orientation of pragmatism with its functional view of the truth."[137] If on Case's part in particular, there is a notable absence of explicit discussion of pragmatism, it is equally true that there are significant, if implicit, thematic parallels between the socio-historical method of Case and American pragmatism. For example, Case would undoubtedly have found himself virtually in full agreement with James' description of the actions of a pragmatist:

---

[136] Pauck, "The Theology of Shailer Mathews."
[137] Meland, "Reflections on the Chicago School," 19.

> A pragmatist turns his back resolutely and once and for all upon a lot of
> inveterate habits dear to professional philosophers. He turns away from ab-
> straction and insufficiency, from verbal solutions, from bad *a priori* reasons,
> from fixed principles, closed systems, and pretended absolutes and origins.
> He turns towards concreteness and adequacy, towards facts, towards action
> and power.[138]

With respect to the character of truth, Case would have joined James and
Dewey in regarding truth not as something already made, but as that which
is in the making. There are no unchanging dogmas. "Truth is *made*, just as
health, wealth, and strength are made, in the course of experience."[139] Truth
is not a question of correspondence between concept and object. On the
contrary, truth is verified by its consequences and the human experience of
these.[140] So Dewey can state: "If the draft is honored, if existences, following
upon the actions, readjust themselves in the way the idea intends, then the
idea is true."[141] As has already been seen, for Case the only basis on which
particular Christian beliefs could be evaluated is whether or not they meet
the needs of their times. So too for James, "Ideas . . . become true just in so
far as they help us to get into satisfactory relations with other parts of our
experience."[142] Case would also have seconded James' statement in "Pragmatism and Religion" that universal conceptions or particular sensations "have,
indeed, no meaning and no reality if they have no use. But if they have any
use they have that amount of meaning. And the meaning will be true if the
use squares well with life's other uses."[143]

Having noted the above thematic similarities with respect to a functional
view of truth, it should also be stated that this formal topic occupies a minimum of Case's time. There is no thoroughgoing precise discussion or systematic philosophical treatment of this approach within Case's work. Certainly the level of critical awareness and specificity which characterized
Case's relationship to German scholarship is not in evidence here. In fact, it
could be argued obversely that had Case been more directly and fully conscious of the writings of James or Dewey, he might have anticipated and
avoided potential philosophical corners or pitfalls.[144] For example, it could

---

[138] William James, "What Pragmatism Means," in *Essays in Pragmatism* (New York: Hafner,
1948) 144.

[139] William James, "Pragmatism's Conception of Truth," in *Essays in Pragmatism*, 168.

[140] Consequences can also be counterposed to originality. So Foster could make the typically
univocal statement in the introduction to his *Finality* that he "sought to write an effective rather than an original book." Cf. Foster, *Finality*, xi.

[141] John Dewey, *Essays in Experimental Logic* (Chicago: University of Chicago Press, 1916)
306.

[142] William James, "What Pragmatism Means," 147.

[143] William James, "Pragmatism and Religion," in *Pragmatism: A New Name for Some Old
Ways of Thinking* (New York: Longmans, 1907) 273.

[144] Some of these corners and pitfalls will be taken up in Chapter VI.

be hypothesized that Case's treatment of the dynamism of change and continuity within the "essence of Christianity" issue might have been significantly improved if he had accepted Dewey's suggestion that essences should be regarded as working hypotheses, until they are confirmed in practice.[145]

The above discussion, even while granting thematic similarities, does not seem to lend itself to a conclusion of direct or explicit influence by American pragmatism upon the socio-historical method of Case. Both the thematic similarities and the pragmatic cast of the socio-historical method might be better attributed either to a general cultural or regional atmosphere or to the indirect influence of pragmatism through such other Chicago figures as Foster, Ames and Haydon.

Conclusion: Possible American Influences

What has gone before in this subsection has served to illustrate the degree to which various American streams of thought and social contexts may have influenced the origination and subsequent shape of the socio-historical method of S. J. Case. With respect to the Yale School, Case's relationship would seem to have been quite similar in nature to that which he had with various German movements. In short, it appears to have been one of informed independence. With respect to American pragmatism, the evidence seems to indicate some generic and thematic similarities while at the same time demonstrating little in the way of scholarly awareness.

In both subsections of this chapter, the conclusion reached about the influences upon the origins of the socio-historical method seems to be that this method cannot be explained by any simple dependence upon any other contemporary line of thought. Nor at the same time does this method occur *de novo* within an intellectual vacuum. The socio-historical method bears important traces of influence from a wide variety of intellectual and social currents from within Germany and America. In every instance, however, it shows itself to be both set apart in some significant respect from these contemporaries and to be possessed of its own distinctive blend of adapted and indigenous elements.

---

[145] This position is not all that far away from Troeltsch's own thought. Cf. Troeltsch, "What Does 'Essence of Christianity' Mean?" 47–50.

VI

CONCLUSION

Today all religious people who lay any claim to culture and education accept *without reserve* the scientific interpretation of the natural world, although they may feel somewhat hesitant about the propriety of its application in the field of religion. . . . The scientific historian cannot allow himself to share even this measure of reserve.

—Shirley Jackson Case

The recent renaissance of interest in the Chicago School and the socio-historical method, as previously outlined in the Preface, has served to underline the necessity of an accurate understanding of the dimensions and workings of this method. Accordingly, the preoccupation of the intervening chapters has been the identification and systematic explication of this method as envisioned and utilized by Shirley Jackson Case.

The socio-historical method was seen to arise from the confluence at the Divinity School of the University of Chicago of the initial dynamics of Harper's impetus toward the democratization of knowledge and Case's subsequent attempt to understand Christianity in an evolutionary manner. In contrast to many European faculties, Harper's disciples strongly opposed any serious dichotomy between the discoveries of academic scholarship in the field of religion and the existential concerns of the pulpit. Behind this, of course, lay the optimistic assumption that the relationship between science and religion was fundamentally a productive one. This in turn placed the Chicago modernists on a clear collision course with the fundamentalists.

For his part, when Case arrived at Chicago, he brought a methodological commitment to empirical scientific history, a neo-Ritschlian assurance that Christianity is a product of an individual's inner reaffirmation of the significance of Jesus, and the conviction that the outward expression of Christianity flows from this inner reaffirmation in response to evolving needs of individuals and changing socio-cultural settings.

Ultimately the socio-historical method as developed by Case attempted to study the empirical history of Christianity as a social movement composed of actual individuals and to understand various Christian productions, especially religious beliefs and theologies, as genetically connected to the inward needs of the members of the movement and to the outward cultural situations. A number of factors were identified as central to the operation of the socio-historical method. Some of these factors were more closely associated with Case's earlier work as a New Testament scholar, such as the "social test," "functional significance," the "didactic character of Jesus" and the "vitalistic nature of Christianity." Other factors in the socio-historical method came more to the fore during Case's work as a church historian, such as "scientific history," "evolutionary development," "genetic connection" and "human activism."

In assessing the origins of the socio-historical method in relationship to already existing theological and historical movements within Europe, Case and most of his Chicago colleagues were seen to have been extremely well informed while maintaining a high degree of independence. Nonetheless, a general anti-philosophical attitude may have led Case to be less well informed on occasion in areas which involved philosophical reflection. Thus with respect to the existing literature centering on the distinction between ideographic and nomothetic methodologies, one might have wished that Case could have been somewhat better informed, if no less independent.

In regard to possible relationships with theological and historical movements within America, there is a notable absence of the same type of informed and explicit discussion which has been already observed with respect to European developments. While one may wish to presume a general influence of the American pragmatists upon Case's socio-historical method, one must still look in vain for any extended analysis of the thought of John Dewey or William James. Such extensive discussion had to await the advent of Henry Nelson Wieman.

Given the preceding information and analysis, it seems clear in assessing the socio-historical method as envisioned and practiced by Shirley Jackson Case that the greatest weakness of the method would seem to be its persistent lack of philosophical circumspection. Nonetheless, this degree of weakness is outweighed by what might be considered to be the greatest strength of the socio-historical method, that is, its functional approach to the history of the beliefs of the Christian *societas*. It is this functionalism which gives the socio-historical method its distinctive ability to explain the genesis and evolution of the radical diversity of beliefs within the same religion.

Failure of Philosophical Circumspection

The lack of philosophical circumspection could be argued to be implicit in Case's generally antagonistic attitude toward philosophy's presence within the historical disciplines, and in his specific unwillingness to examine various underlying assumptions within the socio-historical method itself. Bernard Meland suggests that it is the prospect of extended reflection separated from social action which is abhorrent to Case and his colleagues: "All modernists within the socio-historical school, in my experience, shared something of this distrust of introspection and reflection dissociated from social thinking and activity."[1]

As has already been demonstrated, Case strenuously delimits the formal use of philosophy and metaphysics within the operations of the socio-historical method. For example, questions of truth or falsity are not to be treated within the boundaries of such a historical method because "strict objectivity demands the exclusion of superhistorical criteria from the field of historical operations, without any intention of excluding them from their own proper sphere."[2] This quote would seem to indicate Case's intent to bracket all philosophical questions temporarily so that he can get on with the business of history. In practice, however, the contrary becomes quite evident. This bracketing in fact excludes only certain philosophical questions and assumptions. Further, these assumptions are not merely excluded temporarily but permanently. At the same time, in Case's use of the socio-historical method, other philosophical assumptions appear regularly inside the declared philosophical brackets.

By way of example, note again the previous quote in which superhistorical criteria are excluded. This exclusion is justified by reference to the standard of "strict objectivity." Even if, for the sake of argument, the possibility of such a standard were conceded, such a notion in itself would have to be based upon a philosophical assumption of the first order. Accordingly, within the very establishing of the groundwork of the socio-historical method, there appears to be an extremely important contradiction: namely, that philosophical considerations are disavowed by reference to a particular philosophical assumption.

Thus as one examines the socio-historical method, it becomes clear that Case's apparent argument for the exclusion of philosophically grounded approaches as such is really an argument for the acceptance of one philosophically grounded approach over another. Isn't this what is at the heart of the ongoing arguments for the rejection of metaphysics in favor of worshiping at the shrine of empiricism, or the rejection of the normative use of the past in favor of the didactic use of the past, or the rejection of essentialism in favor of functionalism? In the end, these philosophical brackets do not result in the preclusion of philosophical premises but rather in the preclusion of a formal or systematic reflection upon those covert philosophical premises which have crept around the edges of these brackets into the socio-historical method.

The lack of adequate philosophical circumspection also contributes directly to Case's unwillingness to examine and assess a number of specific assumptions underlying the socio-historical method. Several of these assumptions prove individually troublesome if not mutually inconsistent. Indeed, in

---

[1] Meland, "A Long Look," 24.

[2] Case, "Historical Study of Christian Doctrine," 153.

the absence of sufficient philosophical reflection, such weaknesses can fester
into larger problems. Thus, a variety of problematic questions remain unre-
solved at the center of the socio-historical method. These include the determination of criteria by which societal needs may be identified and assessed,
the resolution of the apparent conflict between relativism and absolutism,
the questioning of the assumption that there is human progress in history,
the problem of providing for continuity within a functional analysis of a
religious movement, the provision for an awareness of the conditionedness of
the socio-historical method itself and determining whether this method embodies an inherent tendency toward historicism. A brief treatment of some
of these unexamined assumptions can serve to illustrate the negative consequences accruing from this lack of philosophical circumspection.

In a short brilliant essay contributed to the Case memorial issue of the
Journal of Religion, Paul Schubert has offered a series of extremely perceptive criticisms of the socio-historical method. While the majority of this essay
praises the advantages of the method, Schubert points to an underlying
inconsistency in Case's theory of knowledge. Although Case was "whole-
heartedly opposed to all forms of absolutist thinking, his own view of history
in its cosmic setting was not free from it."[3] When confronting and utilizing
historical sources, he was an empiricist and a relativist. However, when Case
moved to statements about the nature of human history, such as its evidenc-
ing of progress, then he "absolutized his empirical judgments."[4] So it is that
Schubert Ogden can maintain that Case throughout his career was "always
drawn to a hard relativism."[5]

This strong optimistic belief in the ongoing progress of the human race
was, of course, a central tenet of modernism. Even though Case is often
critical of such a progress motif when it occurs in the historical analysis of
others, in the end, he himself is a meliorist, finding the past marked definitely by "progressive development."[6] In the last two thousand years,

> . . . a gradually enlarging circle of mankind has learned to cherish ways of
> living that exemplify honesty, justice, and brotherly kindness. Men have
> caught new visions of what it means to cultivate both individual and social
> righteousness. They have been learning to make life conform to the new
> knowledge about God's universe that modern science has revealed, and in
> the light of this wisdom they have been able to take their place more intelli-
> gently and effectively as fellow workers with God in the daily affairs of hu-
> man living.[7]

[3] Paul Schubert, "Shirley Jackson Case, Historian of Early Christianity: An Appraisal,"
Journal of Religion 19 (1949) 35.

[4] Ibid., 37.

[5] Schubert Ogden, Discussion Vanderbilt Conference, 1969, privately possessed tape.

[6] Case, *History*, 148.

[7] Ibid., 217. For an example of this meliorism applied specifically to the future, see below,
143.

There is nothing in this quote which would indicate that it was written during World War II. A slight hint might be found several lines farther on within this text in a reference to "evil men have multiplied their aggressions." Even such evil as this, however, is viewed as an Augustinian opportunity from which good may come. It is under the specter of crisis and strain that "goodness always thrives best." Futher reassurance can be found in the belief that behind the instrumentality of human beings in this struggle for progress lies the will of God and "limitless time."[8]

In contrast to the dictum that goodness always thrives best in adversity, Langdon Gilkey, the son of Case's colleague Charles Gilkey, interred in China with Christian missionaries at the same time, would later reflect: "Nothing indicates so clearly the fixed belief in the innate goodness of humans as does this confidence that when the chips are down, and we are revealed for what we really are, we will all be good to one another. Nothing could be so totally in error."[9]

In the face of growing sentiment toward neo-orthodoxy, Case and his Chicago colleagues exhibit little sense of finitude, sin, tragedy or despair but maintain their modernist belief in the effectiveness of human activity in achieving the progress of mankind. Within Case's works there is minimum provision for irrational or demonic forces in nature. In these ways, it may be true to say that the modernists provided a much less active role for corruption and sin than did their social gospel predecessors.

Robert Hutchinson in his *The Modernist Impulse in American Protestantism* sees Case as one of the few liberal modernists who, in the face of World War II, continued to tolerate no pessimism within his overall belief in progress. This seems to distinguish modernism in general and Case in particular from those liberals who adjusted to the times by incorporating a greater role for the sinfulness of humanity and the ambiguity of progress.[10] So it is that a liberal like Paul Tillich, according to Martin Marty, could come to realize "that a realistic view of life 'includes a consciousness of the corruption of existence,' something which Rauschenbush held in a modified form but the modernists tended to let slip."[11]

A greater degree of philosophical circumspection might have challenged this modernist belief in progress. By the same token, a more consistent self-application of the contextual approach of the socio-historical method itself might have insisted that such a belief in progress was conditioned inevitably by and related inextricably to a given socio-historical context. It would have been a healthy realization for the modernists in the Chicago School to have reflected on the degree to which they "shared with the business mind and

---

[8] Case, *History*, 217.

[9] Langdon Gilkey, *Shantung Compound* (New York: Harper & Row, 1966) 92.

[10] Hutchinson, *Modernist Impulse*, 287, 295, 309.

[11] Martin Marty, *Righteous Empire* (New York: Dial Press, 1970) 243.

the temperamental preoccupation with well-being a stubborn optimism that brooked no traffic with pessimism."[12]

An additional assumption of modernism and the socio-historical method, also not subject to any appreciable degree of philosophical reflection, was "scientific thinking" or the "scientific method." Enshrined in a sacrosanct atmosphere, these phrases are not open to any serious challenge, let alone a precise detailing of their meaning:

> Today all religious people who lay any claims to culture and education accept *without reserve* the scientific interpretation of the natural world, although they may feel somewhat hesitant about the propriety of its application in the field of religion. . . . The scientific historian cannot allow himself to share even this measure of reserve.[13]

While Case claims to be unwilling to grant any Christian belief in the past an absolute or normative character, he is eager at the same time to grant normativeness to the scientific method in the present. Scientific knowledge "must be allowed to displace or supplement even the most revered dogmas in every area of cultural life."[14]

In general, Case's notion of science is a very generic one which seldom goes explicitly beyond the injunctions to be empirical and inductive. Implicitly the model of science utilized seems to be a somewhat romantic one along the general lines of a deistic Newtonian model. Accordingly, the relationship between science and religion is viewed as inherently cooperative and productive. Obviously, for Case an empirical and inductive method does not in itself exclude the experience and analysis of spiritual realities. Thus, the scientific enterprise does not terminate in any form of atheism or skepticism but, on the contrary, serves to increase the need for the religious quest: "Science has not removed all of the imponderables from religion; it has only increased their immensity."[15] As scientific knowledge "grows from more to more, the reverence of mankind will ever enlarge."[16] This is precisely the reverse of the view expressed best by Sigmund Freud two decades earlier in his *The Future of an Illusion* (1927). Here the relationship between the scientific enterprise and religion is an antagonistic and inverse one, so that as the one increased the other must necessarily decrease.[17] However, for Case, the relationship is a complementary and direct one, so that as science increases so too will religion.

---

[12] Meland, "Genius of Protestantism," 286.

[13] Case, *History*, 203–4. Italics added for emphasis.

[14] Ibid.

[15] Ibid., 205.

[16] Ibid., 210. This is a good example of Case's meliorism with respect to the future.

[17] Sigmund Freud, *The Future of an Illusion*, trans. W. D. Roson-Scott (New York: Doubleday & Co., 1964) 86, 89–92.

At the base of this direct relationship between science and religion lie both the notion of human instrumentality and natural law as revelatory of God's will. For Case, instrumentality allows God to be immanently present in human creative processes while placing responsibility for the future of the world in humanity's hands. It is this notion of instrumentality, as observed previously, which permits Case to maintain a holistic view of history instead of having to divide it into dual realms of sacred and secular. As with Stoicism, natural laws also serve here to unite these realms. In discovering the inexorable laws of nature, the scientific method has access to God: "Thus derived, the laws of history are laws of the universe, and the laws of the universe are the laws of God."[18]

Had Case explored other models of science besides this Newtonian one this might have occasioned somewhat more cautious claims for the latter. Had this occurred, appropriate allowance could have been made for dysfunctional or negative relationships between some models of science and some models of religion. This is not to imply that one should never adopt a Newtonian model of science, a Stoic notion of natural law, or a Thomistic view of instrumentality. Rather, it is to suggest that the adoption of any such position should occur against the backdrop of a critical assessment of the various available options. This examination can provide the opportunity for both the discovery of inherent inadequacies in given options and for designing sufficient compensation for such inadequacies. On the other hand, the lack of such a critical review increases the possibility that simplistic, anachronistic or inaccurate models may be employed.

By concentrating on the functionalism factor and rejecting almost everything which hints of being essentialistic or nomothetic, Case pares away many of the traditional bases by which coherence or continuity can be provided within the ongoing history of the Christian movement. To some degree, one may be left with a picture of Christianity as powered from within, not by any essential and continuing content but rather by a type of general vitalism. It is this force which empowers Christianity in its continuous process of adaptation to changing cultural situations. Thus, that which gives rise to Christianity's particular coherence or perpetuity seems traceable not to any specific content but rather to the quality or degree of the power of adaptability:

> It was not any supposably [*sic*] static feature of Christianity, remaining absolutely unaltered by time, that gave it perpetuity. Rather its permanence was insured by the facility, more or less great according to circumstances, with which the movement from time to time produced such concrete features of dogma, ritual, organization, and action as served the needs of the hour. Christianity triumphed not by virtue of one or another item that emerged in

---

[18] Case, "Historical Study of Religion," 16–17. Cf. Case, *History*, 205–210.

> the course of its evolution, but as a movement taken in its entirety and ever
> developing by the intricate process of vital social experience.[19]

This quote is reminiscent of the earlier discussion of Ernst Troeltsch's "productive power" within the essence of Christianity. Nonetheless the impression left by Case is that Christianity is powered inwardly by this vitalism which allows it to adapt as needed to meet changing external circumstances but which does not produce any specifically stable or normative content. Continuity between the beliefs and activities of one generation and the next would seem to be largely dependent upon the handing over of this power of adaptability. In other words the content of Christianity seems fundamentally a question of external specification of this internal vitalism.

Reinhold Niebuhr criticized Case's socio-historical method on this point. Delivering the Rauschenbusch lectures the year after Case, Niebuhr stated that Case fell victim to the liberal illusion that the ethic of the Gospel was a prudential ethic in which "necessary compromises are regarded merely as adjustments to varying ages and changing circumstances." For Niebuhr, this was to miss the specific uniqueness of the Christian ethic.[20]

As has been observed earlier, Case was quite wary of claims made for any specific Christian belief as to its uniqueness or perpetuity lest this lead inevitably toward an essentialism in which the influence of historical contexts is minimized or restricted to accidental matters or marginal areas somewhere between content and context. At this point Case seems to exhibit an awareness of some of the possible philosophical consequences of such a model. Nonetheless, this philosophical consciousness was not broad enough to encompass reflection on the reverse possibility. This might have raised the question whether such a serious respect for the conditionedness supplied by historical contexts could tend inevitably toward an existential reductionism in which any specific or unique content of Christianity is virtually removed. The failure to address this question may be said to constitute a serious flaw within the socio-historical method.

This general lack of adequate philosophical circumspection can have theological consequences as well. By placing philosophical questions formally beyond the pale of the socio-historical method, this approach can become antagonistic toward theological reflection insofar as such reflection is grounded in philosophical language or perspectives. Furthermore, if one holds the position that philosophical precision and clarity are essential to any theological enterprise, then this theological enterprise is essentially impeded or flawed by Case's design and practice of the socio-historical method. This is very likely what Wilhelm Pauck meant when he stated: "The weakness of

---

[19] Case, *Social Origins*, 249.

[20] Reinhold Niebuhr, *An Interpretation of Christian Ethics* (New York: Harper & Brothers, 1935) 61–62.

Case's procedure was that he neglected to take seriously the *theological* aspects of church history, and of the method of studying it. His books on Jesus show this most plainly."[21]

Some of the possible roots of Case's bias against taking philosophy and philosophically refracted theology as seriously as he took history and historically refracted theology have been examined. These include the early Ritschlian and Neo-Kantian background of many Chicago figures as well as the disruption which philosophy's relentless search for the truth, particularly in the hands of Foster, could cause vis-à-vis the goals of modernism. Not only did this lack of philosophical circumspection limit the viability of the socio-historical method, but also within the context of the ongoing history of the Divinity School, it foretokened a later time of philosophical counterreaction with a consequent shunting aside of historical questions to the isolated corner formerly reserved for philosophical questions.

The seeds of this counterreaction can be found within this same Chicago group at this period. Thus, G. B. Smith calls for a greater critical philosophical circumspection. In reviewing Alfred North Whitehead's *Science and the Modern World* in May 1926, he commented:

> Those who feel that the health of religious interpretation demands something more than an analysis of states of consciousness or an investigation of social phenomena will be heartened by Professor Whitehead's trenchant criticism of certain aspects of modern scientific procedure. By means of an illuminating historical survey, he points out the persistent anti-philosophical temper of science. The consequence is the retention of philosophically naive conceptions of reality.[22]

To their credit many of Smith's colleagues were reading Whitehead's works during this period, especially *Religion in the Making*. Reflecting the historical orientation of the School, however, it is not surprising that most view Whitehead considerably less enthusiastically than Smith. According to Meland, even though Smith found strong affinities between Whitehead's ideas and his own, Case thought Whitehead but one more example of a "metaphysically burdened philosopher" creating unnecessary problems. Mathews found *Religion in the Making* unintelligible but conceded that possibly the "fault was in ourselves."[23] Perhaps, seeking a safety check against their own orientation, the Divinity School invited Henry Nelson Wieman, who had just published a work on Whitehead's method, to explicate Whitehead's thought to the assembled Divinity School faculty and students in May 1926. It is a testimony to just how well Wieman succeeded in

---

[21] Letter, Wilhelm Pauck to William J. Hynes, April 2, 1971.

[22] G. B. Smith, Review of Alfred North Whitehead, *Science and the Modern World*, in *Journal of Religion* 6 (1926) 313.

[23] Arnold, *Near the Edge of Battle*, 65.

doing just this that he was offered an appointment to the Divinity School for the following year. His position was Professor of Christian Thought and Philosophy of Religion. The latter portion of this title had not been used within the Divinity School since Foster's transfer to the Philosophy Department in the early 1900s. Wieman's appointment and title mark the figurative and literal return of philosophical reflection and philosophically grounded theology into the good graces of the Divinity School. According to one recent interpretation, for Wieman, "his work at Chicago was an attempt to call the School back to theological concerns which had been jettisoned by the modernism of the other Chicago figures before him."[24]

This readmittance of philosophy and philosophically refracted theological endeavors was to have significant repercussions within the ongoing history of the Divinity School. By hindsight, it can be said to have signaled the beginning of the end of that Chicago School which was characterized by the practice of a common socio-historical method. In a classic pendulum metaphor, the previous tendency to place philosophical questions beyond the pale of the socio-historical method led in turn to the diametrically opposite situation in which philosophy and philosophically related enterprises now reigned supreme with historical disciplines placed outside the new pale. The effect was the dissociation of "theological interpretation from the guidance of . . . technical historical disciplines."[25] Within the decade following Case's retirement from the deanship in 1938, this methodological dissociation was underlined by a significant attrition in the historians whom Case had so diligently gathered at Chicago.[26]

What occurs at Chicago during this period is that a thesis which had virtually excluded its supposed antithesis is in turn virtually replaced by this antithesis. Through the 1950s, at least, there is little evidence of anyone proposing any synthesis between the earlier socio-historical method and the later philosophical concerns in such a way as to catch successfully the corporate interest of the Divinity School faculty with an intensity equal to that of either its thesis or antithesis. Thus, not only was the socio-historical method itself by-passed, but the possibility of its inclusion in a synthesis was also neglected seriously. When a significant renaissance of interest in the socio-historical method began to occur in the late 1960s, Sidney Mead remarked:

---

[24] Larry E. Axel, "Modernism and the 'Chicago School of Theology,'" Address delivered to the National American Academy of Religion, 1974, privately possessed copy, 9. Drawing upon an unpublished intellectual autobiography by Wieman, Axel maintains that Wieman saw his work as "a solitary reform at Chicago. Wieman wanted to determine the nature of God and the proper means of adaptation to that reality; he did not wish to study human ideals or the socio-historical development of religious systems. Consequently, in his autobiography, he has drawn sharp contrast between his own work and that of the 'Chicago School.'" Axel, "Modernism," 28.

[25] Meland, "A Long Look," 26. Arnold aptly titles this new era in the Divinity School as the period of the "philosophico-theological method." Arnold, *Near the Edge of Battle*, 60ff.

[26] See Chapter I.

"For about 30 years I have lamented the way that young neo-orthodox men just pushed aside what the Chicago School represented, and I am happy to have lived long enough to see a revival of interest in it."[27]

Success of the Functional Study of Religions

The greatest strength of the socio-historical method lies in its distinctive capacity to analyze and interpret religious beliefs in their functional relationship both to the underlying religious *societas* and to the surrounding cultural environment. In this the socio-historical method may be regarded as providing a particularly viable and imaginative method for the analysis and interpretation of religious literature, the chronicling of evolving religious beliefs, the writing of social religious history, and the doing of certain types of historical theology.

The impact and significance of the socio-historical method for the doing of social religious history might be best compared with the parallel effect of James Harvey Robinson's *The New History* (1912) on the doing of social secular history. Each resulted in the respective redefinition of how history was to be understood in the religious and secular realms. For Robinson, secular history is not to be limited merely to "past politics."[28] So too for Case, religious history is not to be limited merely to "past dogma." Both men conceive of history as not coextensive with the beliefs and actions of a few great persons in certain prominent positions but rather the combined beliefs and actions of ordinary individuals. It follows that history, neither in its making nor recording, must be thought to be restricted solely to the literate few but must be extended to include the non-literate and their non-literary records. This latter stress, of course, automatically impels the historian into such other disciplines as art history, anthropology and psychology.

Identifying history with humanity's social experience, both Robinson and Case effected a fundamental shift away from the exclusivity of institutional or ideological history toward the inclusivity of social history. In this way both scholars anticipated the programs of such groups as the American radical historians or the French L'Annales with their calls for history to be written "from the bottom up," to incorporate a wider and more empirical approach to previously ignored or disenfranchised sectors and to employ less frequently used literary and non-literary sources.[29] In this enterprise,

---

[27] Letter, Sidney Mead to William J. Hynes, April 17, 1970. Mead has a very dim view of both neo-orthodox and process theologians and he tends to identify the two groups when speaking of this period at Chicago. See Mead, "Character and Continuity," 26. For an analysis of the similarities of these groups at Chicago, see Meland, "A Long Look," 25.

[28] James Harvey Robinson, *The New History: Essays Illustrating the Modern Historical Outlook* (New York: Macmillan & Co., 1912) 1–69.

[29] For an example of the approach of the American radical historians, see Jesse Lemisch, "Present-Mindedness Revisited: Anti-Radicalism as a Goal of American Historical Writing Since World War II," Paper delivered to the American Historical Association, Washington, D.C.,

Robinson and Case are ultimately urging the very redefinition of the historian's central task itself.

Neither really believed that a fully comprehensive social history could be recaptured, let alone written, in either the secular or the religious realm. Thus, if one redefines the task of the historian of Christianity as not the recovery of the history of dogma or doctrines but the recovery of the history of the religous experiences of Christians, the difficulty and enormity of the task is immediately self evident. Accordingly, there must be the recognition that it is fundamentally impossible to recover either one's total secular or religious social history. The point is not, however, to propose merely the impossible. It is rather that by making social history the goal which the historian attempts to reach, even if imperfectly, important sectors and sources can be progressively and systematically incorporated into the process of historical investigations.

In the end what distinguishes Case's socio-historical method from Robinson's social history is the former's utilization of the "functional factor." While aspects of the functional motif can be found within Robinson, it never becomes as pivotal for Robinson as it was for Case.[30] The latter views all religious rituals, beliefs, theologies, structures, doctrines and dogmas as functional products of Christianity in different environments. No one product has permanent validity. The continued existence of any given Christian product is determined by whether or not it is able to meet the functional needs of the next generation of believers. Thus, this functional factor typifies Case's socio-historical approach far more than it does Robinson's method. If one were forced to select only one of the variety of factors previously identified with Case's method, the most representative choice would be the functional factor.

In his own use of the functional approach to interpret both the literature and social history of Christianity, Case also parallels the use of a similar method within the relatively new discipline of anthropology. More significantly, Case may have been the first to apply such a method specifically to Christianity, anticipating subsequent developments within anthropology. In 1916, Bronislaw Malinowski, one of the foremost developers of anthropology, particularly functional anthropology, wrote his seminal essay entitled "Baloma: the Spirits of the Dead in the Trobriand Island." At the close of

---

1969. For an example of the work of L'Annales school as applied to religious history, see Jean Delemeau, *From Luther to Voltaire: A New Look at the Catholic Counter Reformation* (Philadelphia: Westminster Press, 1979).

[30] On occasion, Robinson's method sounds quite similar to Case's pleas for a didactic use of the past: "We adjust our recollection to our needs and aspirations, and ask from it light on the particular problems that face us. History, too, is in this sense not fixed and immutable, but ever changing. Each age has a perfect right to select from the annals of mankind those facts that seem to have a particular bearing on the matters it has at hand." Robinson, *New History*, 134–35.

the essay, he decried the supposed fact that this method had thus far been used in application only to primitive religions and that as yet no one had sought to study Christianity in such a manner.[31] Unfortunately, Malinowski was unaware of the publication two years earlier of Case's own functional study of Christianity, *The Evolution of Christianity: A Genetic Study of First Century Christianity in Relationship to Its Religious Environment*. It is this functional approach to religious beliefs which continues to give Case a contemporary flavor in comparison with more recent literature in functional anthropology, such as Clifford Geertz's seminal essay, "Religion as a Cultural System."[32] In fact, a number of potentially positive correlations between the socio-historical method of Shirley Jackson Case and contemporary methodological developments within functional and cultural anthropology suggest themselves to the interested and inquisitive student for the future.

This functional motif within the socio-historical method has a very straightforward secular cast to it. It is secular in the way in which James Hastings Nichols speaks of the post-Enlightenment West as attempting to reach supposed secular neutrality in the sciences, the humanities, and politics.[33] The goal was to practice the same secular method whether it be in the writing of profane or religious history. This secularist cast often impressed and affected significantly those who encountered it at Chicago:

> This present revival of interest in "the Chicago School" suggests to me a growing awareness that some of these men who not only talked about but lived in the secular city, were thoroughly "modern," and formulated some of the basic questions confronting the faith in the modern world. My personal testimony would be that after being exposed to Case and his cohorts in the late 1930's, the post-Christian, post-Protestant era, the secular city, the death of God, and the other recent fads have seemed to me somewhat quaint and highly abstract notions.[34]

The socio-historical method with its functional approach and secularist cast has been seen to have been articulated lucidly and employed ably by Case. Inherent flaws in the method outweigh neither the quality nor the number of works in which Case utilized this method. Perhaps this is why

---

[31] Bronislaw Malinowski, "Baloma: the Spirits of the Dead in the Trobriand Island," in *Magic, Science and Religion* (New York: Anchor Books, 1954) 273, n. 76.

[32] Clifford Geertz, "Religion as a Cultural System," in *The Interpretation of Cultures* (New York: Basic Books Inc., 1973) 87–125.

[33] James Hastings Nichols, *History of Christianity 1650–1950: Secularization of the West* (New York: Ronald Press, 1956) 6ff.

[34] Mead, "Character and Continuity," 27. Mead goes on to suggest that those trained in Chicago modernism have been living in secularity for some time and that the recent fads in secularism are really only epigenetic of a reconsideration process by those who pursued the neo-orthodox option in the past.

one of the strongest critics of Case's lack of philosophical circumspection, Paul Schubert, can still conclude:

> It is no exaggeration to say in conclusion that Case's published works, taken in their entirety, are an original and impressive statement of a functionalist and vitalist conception of reality which surpasses many more formal, philosophical expressions of this view. Case's work owes its persuasive excellence and its enduring significance to the fact that as a historian he brought to his work a balanced sense of the possibilities and limitations of "actual people," and a keen appreciation of the concreteness and complexity of reality. In the art of applying these qualities to historical interpretation, Shirley Jackson Case the historian of early Christianity had no peer.[35]

There are particular advantages which this functionalism motif can bring to both the writing and teaching of historical realities. The socio-historical method is rooted in a commitment to bridge functionally the supposed gaps between the apparently antiquarian historical past and the rootless present. The Chicago School sought to produce not scholarship for its own sake but scholarship whose immediate by-product was relevant to the concerns of the present. Thus, Case was as dedicated to thorough scholarship as he was to the demonstration of the relevancy of the past to the present. For most exercises in relevancy, especially those conducted in isolation from the past, time is the greatest enemy. However, in this particular instance, Case's socio-historical method and its results have stood up rather well to this test and considerably better than most such efforts.

Finally, this functional approach significantly extended Harper's concern that American scholarship exist in service to the general community and that its results be available in an intelligible and relevant manner to all equally. It is this commitment to improve the state of public knowledge which leads the Chicago School into a running battle with the fundamentalists in the 1920s. For many, this was not merely a battle but a war. It was a war for the "lay mind" in which Chicago made use of the "lay weapon"— the secular functionalism of the socio-historical method. This method proved itself a particularly effective debate vehicle by which to defeat those who denied the inherent conditionedness of all expressions of Christian beliefs. It was, as Sidney Mead has observed, "the right war, at the right time, with the right weapon."[36]

---

[35] Schubert, "Shirley Jackson Case," 46.
[36] Mead, "Character and Continuity," 26.

SELECTED RESOURCES

Works by Shirley Jackson Case

The Book of Revelation: An Outline Bible-Study Course of the American Institute of Sacred Literature. Chicago: University of Chicago Press, 1918.

The Christian Philosophy of History. Chicago: University of Chicago Press, 1943.

Christianity in a Changing World. New York: Harper & Brothers, 1941.

The Evolution of Early Christianity: A Genetic Study of First-Century Christianity in Relation to Its Religious Environment. Chicago: University of Chicago Press, 1914.

Experience with the Supernatural in Early Christian Times. New York: Century Co., 1929.

Highways of Christian Doctrine. Chicago: Willett, Clark & Co., 1936.

The Historicity of Jesus: A Criticism of the Contention That Jesus Never Lived, a Statement of the Evidence for His Existence, an Estimate of His Relation to Christianity. Chicago: University of Chicago Press, 1912.

Jesus: A New Biography. Chicago: University of Chicago Press, 1927.

Jesus Through the Centuries. Chicago: University of Chicago Press, 1932.

Makers of Christianity: From Jesus to Charlemagne. New York: Holt & Co., 1934.

The Millennial Hope: A Phase of War-Time Thinking. Chicago: University of Chicago Press, 1918.

The Origins of Christian Supernaturalism. Chicago: University of Chicago Press, 1946.

The Revelation of John: A Historical Interpretetion. Chicago: University of Chicago Press, 1919.

The Social Origins of Christianity. Chicago: University of Chicago Press, 1923.

The Social Triumph of the Ancient Church. New York: Harper Brothers, 1933.

Articles by Shirley Jackson Case

"Authority for the Sacraments." *Biblical World* 29 (1907) 357–60.

"Contributions of the Yale Divinity School to Theological Literature." *The Centennial Celebration of the Founding of the Yale Divinity School*. New Haven: Yale University Press, 1922, 19–24.

"Education in Liberalism." *Contemporary American Theology*. Edited by Vergilius Ferm. New York: Roundtable Press, 1932, 1.107–21.

"The Historical Method In The Study of Religion." *Yale Divinity Quarterly* 4 (1908) 121–133.

"The Historical Study of Christian Doctrine." *Iliff Review* 2 (1945) 157–67.

"The Historicity of Jesus." *American Journal of Theology* 15 (1911) 2–42.

"Jesus and Historical Inquiry." *Biblical World* 34 (1909) 75–78.

"Jesus and Sepphoris." *Journal of Biblical Literature* 44 (1926) 14–22.

"The Life Of Jesus During The Last Quarter Century." *Journal of Religion* 5 (1925) 561–75.

"Living in the Garden of Eden." *Crozer Quarterly* 21 (1944) 134–40.

"The Lure of Christology." *Journal of Religion* 25 (1945) 157–69.

"Modern Belief About Jesus." *Biblical World* 37 (1911) 7–18.

"The New Testament Writers' Interpretation of the Old Testament." *Biblical World* 38 (1911) 98–102.

"Paul's Historical Relation to the First Disciples." *American Journal of Theology* 11 (1907) 269–86.

"The Premillennial Menace." *Biblical World* 52 (1918) 16–23.

"The Rehabilitation of Church History in Ministerial Education." *Journal of Religion* 4 (1924) 225–42.

"The Rehabilitation of Pharisaism." *Biblical World* 41 (1913) 92–98.

"The Religion of Jesus." *American Journal of Theology* 14 (1910) 234–52.

"The Religious Meaning of the Past," *Journal of Religion* 4 (1924) 576–91.

"The Study of Early Christianity." *A Guide To The Study Of The Christian Religion*. Edited by G. B. Smith. Chicago: University of Chicago Press, 1916, 241–346.

"Was Christianity A New Religion?" *Biblical World* 31 (1908) 417–27.

Book Reviews by Shirley Jackson Case

Review of Burnett H. Streeter's *The Four Gospels: A Study of Origins* and Erich Fascher's *Die formgeschichtliche Methode. Journal of Religion* 5 (1925) 428–31.

Review of Albert Day's *Jesus and Human Personality* and Rudolf Bultmann's *Jesus and the Word. Journal of Religion* 15 (1935) 82–86.

Review of C. C. McCown's *The Search for the Real Jesus. Journal of Religion* 21 (1941) 57–59.

Archives—The University of Chicago

American Institute of Sacred Literature. Letter File.

Burton, Ernest DeWitt. Letter File.

Divinity School Correspondence. Letter File.

Garrison, Winfred Ernest. "Shirley Jackson Case as a Churchman." Memorial Service, University of Chicago, 21 January 1948.

Goodspeed, Edgar J. Letter File.

Journal of Religion. Letter File

McNeill, John T. "Shirley Jackson Case as an Historian." Memorial Service, University of Chicago, 21 January 1948.

Mathews, Shailer. Letter File.

Sweet, William Warren. Letter File.

————, "Shirley Jackson Case: At Home and in His Study." Memorial Service, University of Chicago, 21 January 1948.

Willoughby, Harold R. "Shirley Jackson Case: His Life and Christian Philosophy." Memorial Service, University of Chicago, 21 January 1948.

Consultation On The Chicago School—
1969 Vanderbilt University Conference

Adams, James Luther. "The Relationship Between The Chicago School And The Continent." Address. Privately Possessed Tape.

Colwell, E. C. "The Chicago School of Biblical Interpretation." Address. Privately Possessed Copy.

Funk, Robert. "The Watershed of the American Biblical Tradition: The Chicago School, First Phase, 1892–1920." Address. Privately Possessed Copy.

Meland, Bernard. "Reflections on the Chicago School." Address. Privately Possessed Copy.

Pauck, Wilhelm. "The Theology of Shailer Mathews." Address. Privately Possessed Copy.

Contemporary Correspondence With Principal Figures

Cadbury, H. J., to William J. Hynes, 4 July 1970.

————, to William J. Hynes, 13 August 1970.

Case, Mrs. Egbert A., to William J. Hynes, 29 February 1969.

Jennings, Louis B., to William J. Hynes, 30 January 1968.

McNeill, John T., to William J. Hynes, 9 May 1970.

————, to William J. Hynes, 17 August 1970.

Mead, Sidney, to William J. Hynes, 17 April 1970.

Pauck, Wilhelm, to William J. Hynes, 2 April 1971.

————, to William J. Hynes, 21 September 1975.

Thrift, Charles T., Jr., to William J. Hynes, 12 March 1968.

————, to William J. Hynes, 2 March 1970.

Other Resources

Ahlstrom, Sidney. "The Problem of the History of Religion in America." *Church History* 39 (1970) 224–35.

Arnold, Charles Harvey. *God Before You and Behind You: The Hyde Park Union Church Through a Century 1874–1974.* Chicago: Hyde Park Union Church, 1974.

Arnold, Charles Harvey. *Near The Edge of Battle: A Short History of the Divinity School and the "Chicago School of Theology" 1866–1966.* Chicago: University of Chicago Divinity School Association, 1966.

Axel, Larry E. "Modernism and the 'Chicago School of Theology.'" Address to the National American Academy of Religion, Washington, D.C., 1974.

Bacon, B. W. "The Teaching Ministry For Tomorrow." *The Centennial Celebration of the Founding of the Yale Divinity School.* New Haven: Yale University Press, 1922, 11–17.

————. "Ultimate Problems of Biblical Science." *Journal of Biblical Literature* 22 (1903) 1–14.

Bainton, Roland. *Yale and the Ministry.* New York: Harper & Row, 1967.

Boorstin, Daniel J. *America and the Image of Europe*. New York: Meridian Books, 1960.

Bowman, Robert Maurice. "Shirley Jackson Case." *The Divinity School News* 24 (1957) 12–13.

Brown, William Adams. Review of *The Guide to the Study of the Christian Religion*. *American Journal of Theology* 22 (1918), 443–47.

Bultmann, Rudolf. "The New Approach to the Synoptic Problem." *Journal of Religion* 6 (1926) 337–62.

Cadbury, Henry J. "Fifty Years of New Testament Scholarship in Retrospect." *Journal of Bible & Religion* 28 (1960) 194–98.

————. Review of Burton Scott Easton's *The Gospel Before The Gospel*. *Journal of Religion* 8 (1928) 628–30.

————. Review of S. J. Case's *Jesus: A New Biography*. *Journal of Religion* 8 (1928) 130–36.

Cauthen, Kenneth. *The Impact Of American Religious Liberalism*. New York: Harper & Row, 1962.

Chadwick, Owen. *From Bossuet to Newman: The Idea of Doctrinal Development*. Cambridge: University of Cambridge Press, 1957.

Colwell, Ernest Cadman. "New Testament Scholarship in Prospect." *Journal of Bible & Religion* 28 (1960) 202–14.

Darrow, Clarence. *The Story Of My Life*. New York: Grosset & Dunlap, 1932.

Dewart, Leslie. *The Future of Belief*. New York: Herder & Herder, 1966.

Dewey, John. *Essays In Experimental Logic*. Chicago: University of Chicago Press, 1916.

Elton, G. R. *The Practice of History*. London: Collins-Fontana, 1967.

Enslin, Morton Scott. *The Prophet from Nazareth*. New York: Schocken Books, 1968.

Fascher, Erich. *Die formgeschichtliche Methode*. Göttingen, 1924.

Foster, George Burman. *The Finality of the Christian Religion*. 2nd Edition. Chicago: University of Chicago Press, 1906.

Funk, Robert. "Shirley Jackson Case: Notes Toward An Appreciation." Address to the National Society for Biblical Literature, New York, 1967.

Gates, Errett. "Another Case of Discipline in the Prussian Church." *American Journal of Theology* 16 (1912) 241–55.

Gerrish, Brian. "Jesus, Myth, and History: Troeltsch's Stand in the 'Christ-Myth' Debate." *Journal of Religion* 55 (1975) 13–35.

Gilkey, Langdon. *Shantung Compound*. New York: Harper & Row, 1966.

Glick, Wayne. *The Reality of Christianity*. New York: Harper & Row, 1967.

Greenfield, Larry. "The Theology of Gerald Birney Smith." Ph.D. dissertation. University of Chicago, 1978.

Harnack, Adolph. *Christianity & History*. Translated by Thomas Bailey Sanders. London: Adams & Charles Black, 1896.

__________. *History of Dogma*. Translated by Neil Buchanan. 7 vols. 3rd Edition. London: Dover Publications, 1961.

__________. *Thoughts on the Present Position of Protestantism*. Translated by Thomas Bailey Sanders. London: Adams & Charles Black, 1899.

__________. *What Is Christianity?* Translated by Thomas Bailey Sanders. New York: Harper & Row, 1957.

Harrisville, Roy A. *Benjamin Wisner Bacon: Pioneer In American Biblical Criticism*. Missoula, Montana: Scholars Press, 1976.

__________. *Frank Chamberlain Porter: Pioneer In American Biblical Interpretation*. Missoula, Montana: Scholars Press, 1976.

__________. "Representative American Lives of Jesus." *The Historical Jesus and the Kerygmatic Christ* by Carl E. Braaten and Roy A. Harrisville. New York: Abingdon Press, 1964, 172–96.

Herbst, Jurgen. *The German Historical School in American Scholarship*. New York: Cornell University Press, 1965.

Hofstadter, Richard. *The Progressive Historians*. New York: Vintage Books, 1968.

Hudson, Winthrop S. *Religion in America*. New York: Charles Scribner's Sons, 1965.

__________. "Shifting Trends in Church History." *Journal of Bible & Religion* 28 (1960) 235–44.

Hutchinson, William R. *American Protestant Thought: The Liberal Era*. New York: Harper & Row, 1968.

__________. *The Modernist Impulse in American Protestantism*. Cambridge: Harvard University Press, 1976.

James, William. *Essays in Pragmatism*. New York: Hafner, 1948.

__________. *Pragmatism: A New Name for Some Old Ways of Thinking*. New York: Longmans, 1907.

Käseman, Ernst. "The Problem of the Historical Jesus." *Essays on New Testament Themes*. Studies in Biblical Theology, No. 41. New York: Allenson, 1964.

Knox, John. "A Few Memories and a Great Debt." *Criterion* 5 (1966) 24–27.

Jennings, Louis B. *The Bibliography & Biography of Shirley Jackson Case.* Chicago: University of Chicago Press, 1949.

————. "Shirley Jackson Case: A Study in Methodology." Ph.D. dissertation. University of Chicago, 1964.

Lessing, G. E. *Lessing's Theological Writings.* Translated by Henry Chadwick. London: Adams & Charles Black, 1956.

Loisy, Alfred. *The Gospel & the Church.* Translated by Christopher Home. New York: Charles Scribner's Sons, 1912.

Loomer, Bernard. "The Federated Theological Faculty." *The Divinity School News* 12 (1946) 1–3.

McCown, C. C. "Shirley Jackson Case's Contribution to the Theory of Socio-Historical Interpretation." *Journal of Religion* 29 (1949) 30–47.

McGiffert, A. C. "Chicago School of Theology." *An Encyclopedia of Religion.* Edited by Vergilius Ferm. New York: The Philosophical Library, 1945.

————. *The Seminary and the War: Address Delivered at the Opening of the 82nd Academic Year.* New York: Union Theological Seminary, 1917.

McNeill, John T. et al., eds. *Environmental Factors in Christian History.* Chicago: University of Chicago Press, 1939.

————, and Gamer, Helena M. *Medieval Handbooks of Penance.* New York: Columbia University Press, 1938.

MacIntosh, Douglas C. "Can Pragmatism Furnish a Philosophical Basis for Theology?" *Harvard Theological Review* 3 (January, 1910) 125–35.

Malinowski, Bronislaw. *Magic, Science & Religion.* New York: Anchor Books, 1954.

Marty, Martin. *Righteous Empire: The Protestant Experience in America.* New York: Dial Press, 1970.

Mathews, Shailer. "The Historical Study of Religion." *Guide to the Study of the Christian Religion.* Edited by G. B. Smith. Chicago: University of Chicago Press, 1916, 19–80.

————. *The Messianic Hope in the New Testament.* Chicago: University of Chicago Press, 1905.

————. *New Faith for Old.* New York: Macmillan, 1936.

————. "A Positive Method for an Evangelical Theology." *American Journal of Theology* 13 (1909) 21–46.

Mead, Sidney. "Character and Continuity." *Criterion* 9 (1970) 25–27.

Meland, Bernard. "The Chicago School of Theology." *Twentieth Century Encyclopedia of Religious Knowledge*. Edited by Lefferts A. Loetscher. Grand Rapids: Baker Book House, 1955, 232–33.

————. "A Long Look at the Divinity School and Its Present Crisis." *Criterion* 1 (1962) 21–30.

————. *Realities of Faith*. New York: Oxford Press, 1962.

Mode, Peter G. *The Frontier Spirit in American Christianity*. New York: Macmillan, 1923.

————. "Revivalism as a Phase of Frontier Life." *Journal of Religion* 1 (1921) 337–54.

"Modernist Would Pull God Off Throne, Riley Avers." *Minneapolis Daily Mirror*, May 24, 1920, 1–2.

Niebuhr, Reinhold. *Faith and History: A Comparison of Christian and Modern Views of History*. New York: Charles Scribner's Sons, 1949.

————. *An Interpretation of Christian Ethics*. New York: Harper & Brothers, 1935.

Nelson, Roland. "Fundamentalism and the Northern Baptist Convention." Ph.D. dissertation. University of Chicago, 1964.

Newman, John Henry. *Certain Difficulties Felt by Anglicans in Catholic Teachings*. 2 vols. London: Longmans & Green, 1888.

————. *An Essay on the Development of Christian Doctrine*. New York: Doubleday & Co., 1960.

————. *Grammar of Assent*. New York: Doubleday & Co., 1955.

Palmer, Richard E. *Hermeneutics: Interpretation Theory in Schleiermacher, Dilthey, Heidegger, and Gadamer*. Evanston: Northwestern University Press, 1969.

Pauck, Wilhelm. *Harnack & Troeltsch: Two Historical Theologians*. New York: Oxford Press, 1968.

Pelikan, Jaroslav. *Historical Theology: Continuity and Change in Christian Doctrine*. Philadelphia: Westminster Press, 1971.

Perrin, Norman. "The Challenge of New Testament Theology Today." *Criterion* 4 (1965) 25–34.

Porter, F. C. "Inquiries Concerning the Divinity of Jesus." *American Journal of Theology* 8 (1904) 9–29.

Riley, W. B. *Inspiration or Evolution*. Cleveland: Union Gospel Press, 1926.

Robinson, James Harvey. *The New History: Essays Illustrating The Modern Historical Outlook*. New York: Macmillan & Co., 1912.

Rylaarsdam, Coert, ed. *Transition in Biblical Studies*. Chicago: University of Chicago Press, 1968.

Sandeen, Ernest R. *The Roots of Fundamentalism: British and American Millenarianism 1800–1930*. Chicago: University of Chicago Press, 1970.

Schubert, Paul. "Shirley Jackson Case, Historian of Early Christianity: An Appraisal." *Journal of Religion* 29 (1949) 15–29.

Scott, E. F. "A Social Interpretation of Early Christianity." *Journal of Religion* 4 (1924) 320–21.

Shuler, Claude Martin. "An Interpretation & Evaluation of the Work of Shirley Jackson Case as a Historian of Early Christianity." Th.D. dissertation. Iliff School of Theology, 1964.

Smith, G. B. *Current Christian Thinking*. Chicago: University of Chicago Press, 1928

Smith, G. B. Review of Alfred North Whitehead's *Science and the Modern World*. *Journal of Religion* 6 (1926) 313–15.

Stone, Irving. *Darrow for the Defense*. New York: Doubleday & Co., 1941.

Storr, Richard J. *The Beginning of Graduate Education in America*. Chicago: University of Chicago Press, 1953.

————, *Harper's University*. Chicago: University of Chicago Press, 1966.

Tillich, Paul. *Theology of Culture*. New York: Oxford University Press, 1964.

Troeltsch, Ernst. *The Absoluteless of Christianity and the History of Religions*. Translated by David Reid. Richmond: John Knox Press, 1971.

————. *Christian Thought: Its History and Application*. London: London University Press, 1923.

————. "The Dogmatics of the Religionsgeschichtliche Schule." *American Journal of Theology* 17 (1913) 1–21.

————. Selected Essays of Ernst Troeltsch. Translated by James Luther Adams and Walter F. Bense. Manuscript.

————. *The Social Teachings of the Christian Churches*. Translated by Olive Wyon. 2 vols. New York: Macmillan, 1931.

————. "What Does 'Essence of Christianity' Mean?" *Ernst Troeltsch: Writings on Theology and Religion*. Translated by Robert Morgan and Michael Pye. John Knox Press, 1977.

Walgrave, Jan. *Unfolding Revelation*. Philadelphia: Westminster Press, 1972.

Wallis, Louis. "The Paradox of Modern Biblical Criticism." *Biblical World* 52 (1918) 41–49.

Weinberg, Arthur and Liza. *Verdicts out of Court*. Chicago: Quadrangle Books, 1963.

Wurster, Stephen H. "The 'Modernism' of Shailer Mathews: A Study in American Religious Progressivism, 1894–1924." Ph.D. dissertation. University of Iowa, 1972.

APPENDIX

Size of Printing Runs of Works of S. J. Case
Published by University Of Chicago Press

Title	Date	Size of Run
Historicity of Jesus	1912	3,000
Evolution of Early Christianity	1914	4,000
Millennial Hope	1918	3,000
Revelation of John	1919	2,000
Social Origins of Christianity	1923	1,500
Jesus: A New Biography	1927	7,500
Bibliographical Guide to the History of Christianity	1931	1,000
Jesus through the Centuries	1932	1,000
Christian Philosophy of History	1943	1,000
Origins of Christian Supernaturalism	1946	1,000

These figures were generously provided by Mr. E. J. Villani of the University of Chicago Press.